Play Your Game NOW!

15 Points to Hitting the Winning Shot in Life

Play Your Game NOW!
15 Points to Hitting the Winning Shot in Life

Copyright © 2021 by Elzora Watkins, Hyattsville, MD.

All rights reserved, including the right to reproduce this book or portions thereof in any form whatsoever. Except as permitted under the U.S. Copyright Act of 1976, the scanning, uploading, and electronic sharing of any part of this book without the permission constitute unlawful piracy and theft of the author's intellectual property. For permission and information about the use of this book, contact Elzora at – **gohealthylife@gmail.com**
ISBN: 97-98598528624

Who is this book for?

This is for those of you who have been rear-ended by life and have found yourselves in a tailspin only to realize that once you've stopped spinning, you're trying to catch your bearings so you can head in the right direction.

This book is not full of directions telling you what to do but mostly questions asking you to think deeply about your life. Ideally, the goal is to help you to figure out what you desire in order to create the life you deserve. I think deep down inside, you already know what that is. That's because *"I believe that the solution is in you!"* To get the most out of this book, get some tea, wine, or whatever, find a quiet spot and chill, make sure you take the time to answer the questions that resonate with you the most. If you are a coach, then these are great exercises to do with your clients or at a retreat. Read and answer the questions so you can find the solutions that lie within.

Are you still wondering if this book is for you?

This is for you if you are tired of getting ready to be ready but finally come to a point where you are really ready now!

This book is for you if you are at a job and have been contemplating about taking the next step to wave your own flag!

This is for you if you are about to retire and want to start thinking about doing that next thing! Start a new chapter!

This is for you who are kind of doing the thing and not sure if you should be doing the thing. I say, go ahead and do the doggone thing!

This is for you if you are tired of watching other people do their thing and knowing that you are capable of doing something wonderful. You were created to do something wonderful!

This is for you because you are ready to make a contribution and share your gifts with the world!

This is for you if you are ready to play your game now!

This is for you because you are ready to play Full Out!

This is for you if you are tired of standing on the outside of the court looking in through thick plexiglass watching other people play their game and are ready to suit up, tie their shoes tightly and get on the court!

If you said yes to two or more statements written above, then…

THIS - BOOK - IS - FOR - YOU!

This book is dedicated to

My husband, my partner in doubles, Christopher Milton Watkins, thank you for your ideas, having my back, and continuous love, and for letting me be who I be. **#LetMeBMe**

Babbie Nalle, my #1 Fan. You were always cheering me on while steering me in the right direction. Thank you for showing me what was possible. Rest in peace mentor. **#I'mpossible**

Mr. Kuo, My Teacher. Thank you for showing me what it means to be an entrepreneur when I was in high school. You taught me to never chase the money and let the money chase me. **#LetThe$ChaseMe**

Bob Yates, my mentor, thank you for the Circle of Champions and for allowing me to see your skills on the court! You showed me that I can get paid for doing what I love! **#GetPaid4DoingWhatILuv**

Melissa Hughes, thank you, COACH, for showing me that I can bring ALL of myself to the table and create MY OWN GAME AND RULES! **#AbundanceIsMyBirthRight**

Malika Staar, thank you for working with me and helping me to get my thoughts on paper and SWING! **#NowThatIKnowBetter**

Mary Dell Bellamy, thank you, Mom, for showing me how to SERVE with love. Rest in peace. **#ServeW/Love**

Play Your Game
Table of Contents

Introduction		8
Point 1	Possess a Positive Play Full Out Attitude	13
Point 2	Learn the Rules	33
Point 3	Assume the Position	37
Point 4	Your Mindset is Key, Not the Score	47
Point 5	You Must Play with Grace and Ease	57
Point 6	Own YOUR Game	63
Point 7	Unless you Swing!	73
Point 8	Reach for it!	79
Point 9	Go Where the Ball is Going	85
Point 10	Action Speaks Louder Than Words	93
Point 11	Make Adjustments	99
Point 12	Enjoy the Game	105
Point 13	Next Level Up!	111
Point 14	Own a Finish Strong Attitude	125
Point 15	Win the Game	133

Introduction

The day started off as a normal fall morning just before work. Playing racquetball with Tracy is not only our girls' bonding time, but it is also a great sounding ground to get out our frustrations and talk about what's upsetting us. It's a time of physical and mental relief and good advice from a friend.

For those that have never played racquetball before, it is almost like tennis, however, your battle is more against a small pink rubber ball hitting off the angles of four - 20-foot-high walls surrounding you under a ceiling as opposed to your opponent on the opposite side of a net dictating which way the ball will go. Racquetball can be played with one, two, or three other people. Each faces the same struggle, the walls, the ceiling, and the abilities of their opponents. Each player uses the walls, ceiling and skills as leverage to keep their opponents from scoring points. Ultimately, you will need 15 points to win a game of racquetball.

As I begin to serve the ball, I reflect on how far our game has progressed over these past few years. Our bodies are more toned. Our endurance has increased. Our swings have improved, and our sense of precision has been sharpened. As the game progresses, my lavender shirt is now dark purple, I can taste the salt from the sweat dripping down the right side of my face. Neither one of us has said a word since the game started except for stating the score before each serve. All you could hear was our sneakers screeching against the floor, the little pink rubber ball bouncing off the floor, walls, and ceiling. Occasionally you would hear a grunt of exhilaration when we take a swing at the little pink rubber ball!

Sometimes life may feel like that little pink ball being smacked around from corner to corner…ricocheting off the banks of the corners of the walls lobbying off the 20-foot-high ceiling. Leading pros and top power-hitting amateurs have been known to hit drive serves regularly in the range of 150–160 miles per hour! Sometimes, situations and circumstances are coming at you fast 160 miles per hour just like that little pink ball, and all you can do is react in hopes that life will allow you to score a point or two.

The key to this game is to focus on one shot at a time!

Your experiences are filled with moments that will forever shape your viewpoint on how to approach life. Life altering decisions that move you in the direction in this game called life. Once you've mastered your internal thoughts, your outside life will change.

With each point scored I saw a correlation to the nuances of life. The pages to this book literally unfolded between those four walls, a ceiling and the hardwood floors of a racquetball court! I had so much fun generating the titles to each chapter and connecting them to life! I missed deadline, after deadline after deadline trying to follow someone else's agenda. I edited, proof read and still found errors. And just when I thought I was done,

one conversation with my coach Dineen, I rearranged each chapter to provide a cohesive flow to my signature program. Although I rearranged each chapter for a more cohesive flow, this book is nonlinear, and you may choose to read the chapters in any order.

I invite you to highlight, write in the margins, and take notes! I even added a few blank pages for you to doodle, draw pictures, diagrams, and or sketches! This book was made for you to PLAY FULL OUT! Research shows that when you draw diagrams and pictures, neuro connection between your hands and your brain causes what you drew to stick and stay with you longer.

This book is about you creating a new game, designing the life you deserve, and hit the ball of your choosing. We all have goals and dreams that spring from within our hearts, and it is my desire to help you think about those goals and dreams by showing you how to overcome the internal resistance that may be keeping you stuck and stopping you dead in your tracks. To be happy you need to live a life of purpose. Happiness is not a goal in and of itself, it is a side effect of doing what you are meant to do in this life. It involves giving your talents and abilities to a cause and a purpose that takes you way beyond yourself!

I am honored you are investing your time to read **Play Your Game NOW.** Whoever thought that a simple game of racquetball could teach me so much about how to navigate life. This one game gave me strategies to win at accomplishing my goals, dreams, and aspirations, and now I bring these same strategies to you in hopes to inspire you to *Play Your Game NOW*. Should you find that this book can help someone, please share what you've learned.

Now, let the game begin!

Point 1
Possess a Positive Play Full Out Attitude

Offensive Shot - an aggressive shot meant to score.

"Always do your best. What you plant now, you will harvest later."
~ Og Mandino~

The Morning Routine

I awake from a night of deep sleep to the sound of the screaming alarm clock on my nightstand. It's 6:15 Thursday morning. As I lie in bed, I could smell coffee brewing in the kitchen down the hall, and the sound of Joe Madison's voice from Chris' cell phone was fading as he climbed the stairs to his man cave to get ready for the day. Chris loves listening to Sirius XM talk radio shows first thing in the morning.

My phone rings, I lean over fumbling through the items on my nightstand and reach for my ringing cell phone. It is my morning wakeup call from Tracy. "Morning Cuz!" Tracy's energetic voice greets me like the autumn sun streaming through the venetian blinds above our queen-sized bed. "I'll be leaving the house in 20 minutes," she said. "Ok, I'll meet you there around 7." I replied. I thought to myself, "not before my morning routine."

Research suggests that a common characteristic amongst successful people is a morning routine. I found some positive energy music on YouTube and lie in bed for another fifteen minutes to do my *'Order of Operations'* **PEMDAS**: Pray, Energy medicine, Meditate, Daydream, Ask, then Send love.

Pray - I believe there is something out there greater than me. I call him God, Jehovah Jireh, Jah! I thank Him for waking me up and allowing me to experience this thing called life. I let Him know how grateful and thankful I am for all the blessings I have and that I trust what He has in store for me. Then I ask Him for His protection and guidance.

Energy medicine - focuses on the energy fields of the body that organize and control the growth and repair of cells, tissue, and organs. I use energy medicine to bring balance, vitality, and energy into my day. I notice that when I remember to do my energy medicine it helps me feel better and provides clarity.

Meditate - I can tell when I don't meditate. I've come to realize that I must first find my center of balance before I go off into the world. You have some people whose main purpose is to knock you off balance. When you first take time to focus on yourself it's easier to stay balanced and if someone attempts to knock you off balance you can quickly bounce back.

I then **Daydream** about what I want to manifest in my life. **This is key!** You have to first visualize and see it in your mind before you can create it. Unfortunately, many people just go through the motions of life with no dream or direction like a broken rutter that can no longer steer a boat. We mindlessly follow information doing what other people are doing. Since we were children, we've been taught to 'follow the leader', walk in a straight line, color within the black thick lines of the coloring book. Even when we were learning how to write, our letters had to be perfectly aligned between the three horizontal dashed lines, not to extend beyond. If you follow all the rules, then you can go to recess and if you did not then there was NO recess for you! Sounds familiar?

Ask for support. Oftentimes we don't ask for support.

Especially those of us who were taught, *"if you want something done right, then you have to do it yourself"*. This message might have been overly prescribed! You may have seen it being played out by your parents. I grew up in a single-family household where I saw my mother do everything. Therefore, I grew up thinking I had to do it all. I am now learning how to make a request and ask for help.

Lastly, I **Stretch and Send Love** out into the universe. Stretching must be good, it's the first thing cats and dogs do when they wake up. I do a couple of good stretches, then as I lie in bed, I send out love like a pebble being tossed in a lake sending out ripples of expanding love. I smile as the melody of the music from my cell phone waffles in the air.

It's time to get up. I jump out of bed, stepping over Sasha, our Yorkie, who is curled up on the multicolored rug on the floor at the foot of the bed. Stuart, our other Yorkie is most likely upstairs in the mancave with Chris. I slipped into my exercise clothes lying neatly on the chair beside an antique dresser I bought from a consignment shop in Mount Rainier and quickly washed my face and brushed my teeth with my less dominant right hand. Jim Kwick suggested that you eat and brush your teeth with your less dominant hand because it's good for your brain. I will be 55 on my next birthday so I like to do things to keep my brain sharp and healthy.

Just before leaving, I run upstairs to give Chris a quick kiss. *"I'm on my way to the gym to play racquetball with Tracy, see you later on today"*. I ran down the steps, grabbed a baseball cap hanging on my closet door, my gym bag, and the vanilla keto shake from the refrigerator I had prepared the previous night to save time and then made a mad dash for my grey 2018 Ford Geo Sport parked outside our Cape Cod. I changed the channel to my favorite station, 91.9 as I turned on to 42nd place.

I rolled down the window to feel the crisp fall air on my face as I sang along to the upbeat contemporary Christian songs, sipping on my shake, as I headed to LA Fitness just a few miles down the road from our home. My favorite song comes on the radio just as I pull up to the gym. I thought to myself *"today's going to be a good day!"* I sit in my car singing to the song until it ends before getting out and grabbing the green gym bag and my racquet from the trunk.

"Good morning, Mrs. Watkins," the attendant greets me from behind the registration desk as he holds the electronic device against the tiny plastic card attached to my keychain. "Good morning," I replied. It is always nice walking into a place where people take the time to greet you by your name. I spot a few familiar faces as I pass the row of treadmills, stationary bikes, and stair masters as I walk to the racquetball courts at the back of the gym. I never really liked treadmills; it feels like I'm a hamster running in one spot. I need outside scenery when I jog. Speaking of scenery, I smile as I pass several fit men of all ages, wearing tank tops, sweats or shorts. Beautiful shades and skin colors of different hues, glistening from an early morning workout. As they work out I hear the sound of a bar bell hitting the rubber mat on the floor and I am reminded of all the reasons why I enjoy coming to the gym.

It's 7:13 and Tracy has already started lifting weights while she waits for me to arrive. I hate it when I'm late. "*Hey Cuz!*" I call Tracy "Cuz" even though we're not really cousins. She and I used to work together at Northwestern High School back in the day when I first started teaching. I threw my gym bag down on the bench and begin to stretch some more before entering the court. As I grabbed my left foot from behind stretching my quads, Tracy was doing her last set of hamstring curls on a nearby machine. She had on a pair of black shorts, some white *tennis shoes*, and a pink shirt. I guess I've been in the DMV area too long... since when do I call "*sneakers*", "*tennis shoes*?"

While Tracy finishes her last set of leg curls, I go onto the court to practice my **wallpaper** and **pinch shots**.

Pinch Shot - a hard and low shot aimed at a front corner, striking the side wall before the front wall.

Wallpaper Shot - a down the line shot that rebound straight and sliding along a side wall, it is a difficult shot to return.

Tracy and I typically play racquetball for about 45 minutes to an hour, then I lift some weights for 20 minutes, jump in the pool to do some laps for maybe 10-15 minutes, shower, dress, then head off to Roosevelt High School across the street where I coach math teachers.

From inside the racquetball court, I see an elderly man who looks like he is in his late sixties working out on a bicep curl machine. You can tell he was a heartbreaker back in the day. He was about 6 foot two, slim built, light-skinned with wavy gray hair, a mustache, and a neatly trimmed beard. He's joined by a brown-skinned lady in her sixties who always wears a pearl necklace with her gym attire. I like seeing my elders still hitting the gym, they inspire me.

Tracy entered the court, and we finally started our game. She served. We rally back and forth chasing the ball trying to make each other run as hard as we can, as fast as we can, each of us are trying to score points. Normally, I would be whipping up on Tracy. She tends to second guess her ability. I have learned throughout these years of playing her, that she typically sikes herself out before she even begins to play. To be honest, I have always used that to my advantage.

Today, there was something different about Tracy. She had a newfound confidence. More than just her stride was different, her attitude was different. Today, she was actually going for it! She quickly moved into position, and she was not afraid to step into her shots. She was fully prepared to challenge her mentor. Zig Ziglar said it best: "Your attitude, not your aptitude determines your altitude."

Today Tracy had me chasing shots. Even when I served, she was connecting with the ball, sending it ricocheting from corner to corner. All the pre-game exercise is working to her advantage because when she called the score before serving, it was 10 to 2...and I was the one who had the 2 points! I am not prepared to lose this game! I came here to win! It dawned on me that if I wanted to win, I had to play full out!

Sometimes life's score totally catches you off guard and becomes a wake-up call. What defines how we handle the twists and turns life throws at us, depends on our preparation. Lack of preparation could derail the game. That is why I wrote this book, to give you some of those secrets that will help you embrace the victory mindset.

So, you may be asking how do you prepare to win your game and play full out?

Life does not just happen. There are a series of actions that take place which lead to results. Success does not just fall into your lap. It takes work, perseverance, tenacity, practice but most important... your mindset and a positive attitude. When you want to go to college or trade school you have to study, maybe take the SATs. When you graduated and want to land a job in your field, you had to create your resume, send it out, then sharpen your interviewing skills. When I joined the army at the age of 34, I had to become physically fit, which led to me running two miles a day, working out and conditioning my body to handle the physical demands of boot-camp. I had to mentally prepare for the challenges ahead and stay positive. Mindset is a key ingredient for preparation!

I'm about to date myself. There is no such thing as luck.

Do you remember the Karate Kid, 'wax on, wax off'? Mr. Miyagi had Daniel LaRusso, the main character, paint his fence, wax his car, and many other chores. Unbeknownst to Daniel, the constant circular and vertical hand motions were just the correct motions that he needed to master a special karate fighting technique! I'm going to ask you two key questions. I want you to take a moment and really reflect on each question.

What are the things you need to do in order to be prepared to play your game full out?

Extra juicy question:
Who do you need to be?

This is not a trick question, but one that will help you analyze where you are right now so that you can know how to get to where you want to go. It is difficult to play any sport or create the life that you want if you are not aware of the preparation it will take to get there.

Coming from a teacher's point of view, education is the foundation for wherever you want to go in life. A solid education, whether it is formal or informal, sets the foundation from which you can build upon to accomplish your goals, dreams and aspirations. Unfortunately, some people think as soon as they finish high school or college that learning stops. In other words, they do not continue to invest in their personal growth and development. Some tend to *swing* randomly at life hoping they will connect and land a shot. Learning or improving on techniques are no longer a priority and many people settle into a status quo level of living, only dreaming of making it big or *hitting* the lottery to get to their next level in life. Even those that achieve some level of success may find themselves stuck at a plateau. That doesn't have to be us. We don't have to accept the status quo. We don't have to accept what life *serves* us!

I grew up in a single-family home. My mother only had a fifth-grade education. She was a maid and use to have to take three busses to get to work. We were on welfare. Our first home was a tiny apartment on the third floor of a row house in North Philly. I remember this apartment so vividly. We had a kitchen, a bathroom and two bedrooms. My mother's bedroom doubled as our living room. My brother and I had to share the smaller middle room.

There were gang wars, teenage pregnancy, old men preying on young girls, drug dealers and a Chinese restaurant, church or bar on every corner. All the odds were stacked against us. But I refused to settle for what life seemed to be serving me at that time. I knew I had to do something different and invest in me.

Wealthy people, champion athletes, or anyone who has accomplished a goal, consistently invest in training, expanding their knowledge, and conditioning their bodies and or their minds to win. These high performers all realize that THEY are their greatest investment. Whatever game you want to play in this life, you must be willing to continue to grow. It is quite clear that you are part of a rare tribe of high performers, or else you would not be reading this book. But it takes endurance. Success is not an overnight victory, it is one built upon preparation, perseverance, follow-thru, mindset and a POSITIVE PLAY FULL OUT ATTITUDE.

Are you ready?

Putting the Good Stuff In

Have you ever heard the phrase, "trash-in trash-out"? When I play racquetball and I've not eaten a good breakfast or properly hydrated, halfway into the game, I feel weak, sometimes even nauseous. I lose energy and focus, which prevents me from performing at 100% of my potential. In other words, I don't have the stamina to continue the game at an optimum level. What you eat and drink not only play a huge role in your endurance as an athlete but also as an employee, employer, and especially an entrepreneur.

That is why it is key to put good stuff in your body. Studies have shown that poor nutrition leads to fatigue, depression, and excess weight. Healthy eating feeds the body as well as the mind.

Good stuff 'in' does not just apply to what you eat. It applies to everything you let enter your receptacles...your ears, eyes, thoughts, and what comes OUT of your mouth.

- What do you listen to?
- Who do you listen to?
- What do you read?
- What do you watch on television?

- How long are you watching television?
- What do you mostly talk about?
- What do you mostly think about?

You can tell the answer to these questions by examining where you are now and what you have accomplished as of today. In other words, the answer to all of these questions is a good indication of where you are headed in life. PERIOD! If you find yourself absorbed in listening to, reading, watching, and thinking negative things, then negativity will overtake your game. However, if you are listening to, reading, watching, and thinking about positive things, then you will find more positive outcomes from your game. The ONLY person who can change the outcome is YOU!

A Good Stretch

Every good athlete starts with some sort of warm-up routine. They stretch their muscles before they start their game. Remember, Tracy was already working out prior to our racquetball game starting. I came into the gym and went straight to the court and stretched. Stretching releases, the stiffness from the muscles and lactic acid build-up from them being in a dormant stage. Stretching makes the muscles more agile. It gets the blood flowing through the body. It prepares the body for the trauma it is about to endure from the physical impact of the abrupt stops and pivots of the game. Before I go onto the court, I make sure that I get a good stretch because the older I get the more I need to stretch.

Lastly, stretching also prevents injury.

What does 'stretching' look like in your life?

Stretching can mean reaching beyond your comfort zone. It starts with a regiment or routine that sets the pace for your day. It may look like you taking a class to learn something new. It may look like you coming out of your comfort zone and trying something new, something different, something out of the ordinary. It may look like you meeting with a coach, eating better, stretching beyond your current comfort zone, and creating a new comfort zone!

I once took a sign language class at First Baptist Church of Glenarden. It really pushed me out of my comfort zone. I had to learn how to communicate with facial expressions, and hand gestures. Finally, stretching looks like you coloring outside the thick lines and creating an original or a masterpiece!

It looks like you PLAYING FULL OUT!

The Right Equipment

To some people, a tennis racket and a racquetball racquet look similar, however, in all actuality, they're not. A tennis racket is longer and heavier, whereas a racquetball racquet is lighter and shorter. I'm not sure if they wear gloves in tennis, but I always wear a glove on my left hand to absorb the sweat from my hand and a pair of goggles to protect my eyes. I typically wear a baseball cap to absorb the sweat. For me, it is functional and cute at the same time.

Think about the equipment you might need to play your game full out. What is the right equipment for you? It depends on the game that you play. In most businesses today your equipment is a phone and a computer. Maybe a microphone, a functioning website, or a camera if you are a photographer. You may need to market your products and services in order to let everyone know how you bring your gifts to the world. I use the NowSite to market my products and services because I have several projects and it allows me to make as many websites as I need with no additional cost! Here is a link to check out all the cool features. **https://nowsite.marketing/?af=SaveMoney**

Whatever "that" thing is you need; you must also realize the most important thing. That YOU ARE THE RIGHT EQUIPMENT! Until YOU show up on the court...until you show up in the room...until you show up to be the solution to the problem, that idea, or bring your gifts to the party, nothing can happen! This means you need to think about how you are showing up in the world. You possess the ability to collaborate, communicate, bring dynamic interpersonal skills, teamwork, creativity, and resilience that no one else can bring to the table in such a way as you can.

The Creator created you with all the right equipment for the job that has been ideally designed for you. Your mess is someone else's message. Your unique experiences can serve as a guidepost to light the way for someone else. Your program, book, invention, or idea may even save someone's life. It is your responsibility to bring your gift to the world. Remember, the world is waiting for you to show up because YOU are the right equipment!

The Right Coach or Mentor

Here is a harsh reality check. Even if you put the right stuff in, did all your stretches, had the best equipment, none of it matters unless you are available for guidance. An expert who has already played the game before, can help you move to the next level. That is where having a coach, a mentor or an advisor is key at helping you start and finish your game strong.

The greatest leaders, CEOs, billionaires, presidents, and athletes all have coaches, trainers, and or advisors. No man is an island in and of themselves. You need someone with wisdom and the right experience to help you chart unchartered territory. Having someone to bounce ideas off, having someone to push you beyond the limits of your mind, having someone to steer you in the right direction can be a powerful tool. Only we know what we have been exposed to, our experiences.

Coaches, mentors, and advisors expose us to new and different perspectives and viewpoints. Great coaches will always guide you to push past what you think you can endure. Great teachers are always going to sharpen your intelligence and great advisors are going to help you avoid pitfalls. Ken Schramm says, *"A smart person learns from his mistakes, but a truly wise person learns from the mistakes of others."* What and who are you learning from? See **Point 13, 'Next Level Up'** to learn more about taking your game to the next level.

Visualize the Win!

Your mind is the command central station for every area of your life. If your mind is off, the body is off, and the spirit is off and mental preparation is key when you are getting ready for ANY game! You must have a clear vision of what winning the game looks like.

A person with a growth mindset typically perseveres and looks at obstacles as a challenge. You need to think about yourself as a winner with a can-do, will-do attitude! In other words, a positive play full out attitude. However, if you take on a defeated attitude, then you've already lost. You have to visualize yourself winning but here is the part that people are seldom taught... You have to then FEEL it! I created a course called *Designing Your Desired Destiny* to guide my clients on a journey of how to visualize, create and design the life they desire and deserve. In this course I show them how visualization creates manifestation. Visualization is more than just placing pictures on a board; it is a road map along with using the right strategies that will drive you to your desired destiny. When you visualize and then feel, synchronicities begin to happen, and things begin to simply work out for you. Visualize and feel are important steps but there is another key step, know that you are worthy to receive what you visualize. Feel free to reach out if you like to *Play Your Game Now* and *'Design Your Desired Destiny'*! See **Point 3, 'Assume the Position'** to learn more about visualizing the win.

Get Ready to Receive

When I was an independent director in a multi-level marketing company, one of the leading guys, Andre, would say. "Get Ready - Get Ready - Get ready! That would always get us all fired up! Anyway, I digressed. Once you've *Designed Your Desired Destiny*, how are you getting ready to receive it? The other day my husband Chris asked me what I would do if I had $1,000,000. I had some ideas. However, I wasn't exactly clear about what I would do with it. I don't know about you, but it bothered me that I did not know what I would do with $1,000,000! I know I'm ready to receive it however, if I don't know what to do with it then it will be easily taken or misused. I had to stop and answer the following questions I am posing to you. You may choose to answer all or just the ones that resonates with you the most.

What would I do with $1,000,000? If a million is too small for you, then $100,000,000.

- Do I know what to do with what I've requested?
- How am I preparing to receive what I've requested?
- Once I've received it, how might it impact my life?
- Who will I be?
- What would I do?
- Where will I live?
- What kind of car will I drive?
- What types of food will I eat?
- Where will I travel?
- Who will I help?
- How will I maintain what I've received?
- Who would I surround myself with?
- What will I do when I receive more!?
- What's stopping me from feeling all this good stuff now?

Feel free to add more questions.

Finally, establishing a morning routine, putting in the good stuff, taking a good stretch, having the right equipment, having the right coach or mentor and being ready to receive, all are great but possessing a positive play full out attitude is paramount!

Extra Credit:

What would it look like for me to play with a play full out attitude?

> *"Prepare in your mind first what you want,*
> *then make sure you know what to do with your request."*
> Elzora Watkins

Point 2
Learn the Rules

Foot Fault – a violation that occurs during the serve, when the server steps outside of the service zone before the served ball has bounced.

> *"To live in a system of free enterprise yet not understand the rules of free enterprise, must be the very definition of slavery."*
> *Andrew Young*

Learn the Rules

When you're serving in racquetball, the rules state you have to serve from within the red lines located in the middle of the court, the serving zone. You can lose a point or lose a turn if you were to step outside of the serving zone. Such as it is in life, you have to play within the boundaries. If you don't know the limits or boundaries, then it is easy for you to step out of bounds and get off course.

Before you can play any games, you must know the rules of the game. Rules, regulations, and guidelines bring structure, boundaries, limits, and is advantageous when playing any game. When in compliance you avoid failures, fumbles, flags on the play, and avoidable setbacks. Understand, the rules are not there to take the fun out of the game but to provide direction, structure, and protection. Oftentimes, breaking the rules can cost you the game. In life, it may cost you money, time, resources, and possibly missed opportunities. Your ability to play by the rules builds character, integrity, and credibility. Cheating lets the universe know you are not ready for the reward of the victory. There are very few shortcuts you can take in life that yield lasting rewards.

Do you know the rules, regulations, guidelines for the game you are playing? Do you know which principles that best match the things you are trying to accomplish in life? Once you identify the strategies, boundaries, and limitations, you can master the objective to win without breaking the rules. The gains are far greater.

Play by the Rules

We have all seen the news reports on how celebrities were all busted for bribing ivy league schools to get their children into those schools. Being able to afford to send the kids to the ivy league schools was not the issue. Those celebrities paid far beyond the cost of tuition to get their children accepted into those schools. The idea to break the institution's Code of Ethics brought about criminal charges. They broke the rules. What cost them, in the long run, was far greater than if their children would have just done the work, made the grades and actually played sports, they claimed that they played. Clearly, they were not playing by the rules for college entry.

Sometimes having a winning advantage and privilege gives people a false sense of entitlement. It makes people believe they are above the law. *"I am rich, so I do not have to follow those rules"*. *"This is my 'deck of cards' so we play the way I want to play"*. *"I am smart, so I don't have to study"*. *"I'm an athlete, the rules don't apply to me."* The list goes on of how people justify their behavior for breaking the law, rules, and regulations.

I taught Tracy how to play racquetball, so I am entitled to win. *Right*? Even though I taught her how to play, I also taught her the rules. She has the power to enact upon those rules for her benefit. Stepping outside the boundaries could cost her the game.

Now, for those rule breakers (like me) who don't like following the rules, then I guess you will have to create the rules for your own game! **Point 15 'Win the Game'** was written with you in mind.

What are four ideas you took from the points in this chapter?

_____
_____
_____
_____
_____
_____
_____
_____
_____

What are some rules you want to create for yourself to live by?

_____
_____
_____
_____
_____
_____
_____
_____
_____
_____

Point 3
Assume the Position

Center Court - the most desirable position to hold on court, midway between the side walls and just behind the five-foot line.

> "Position yourself well enough, and circumstances will do the rest"
> Mason Cooley

Act Like You Already Got It! In other words, Act Like You Know!

When my friend Angie's son was accepted to a prestigious school, Angie and her husband was super excited. However, the school was 45 minutes away from their home in Jersey. Angie would have to drive to Duke's new school twice each day. Angie and her husband decided to sell their home and move to the township near Duke's new school. They found a luxury apartment that was not only close to her son's school but was perfect for Angie to have conferences and retreats for her clients. The apartment was sexy! Inside, there was a movie room and three rooms to hold meeting. On the top floor was a penthouse space overlooking the city. In the courtyard there were two fire pit areas surrounded by colorful seats. There were six gas grills and even a pool!

Every night Angie would envision herself waking up in her new apartment. She saw herself conducting retreats and workshops in the luxurious conference space. She even enrolled Duke into visualizing the move! Daily, she would ask Duke to show her how he would walk in the lobby. Duke would throw his sweater over his left shoulder and strut across the floor with his head held high. Duke would then imagine himself making hot chocolate from the beverage machine in the lobby. Although this was a big audacious scary move, Angie took a chance, a leap of faith and turned her dream into a reality. Not only does Angie and her family get to enjoy this amazing space, but her clients get to learn how to build their brand! She currently planning her first conference in October!

You have to assume the position in your mind first before you physically get there! That's what Angie did! As I would serve the ball, I would envision a higher score. I would think to myself 3-10. I would visualize myself winning. One point at a time.

My vision journals allowed me to pull the dreams from my head and lay them out in living color! The journal allowed me to visualize, prepare my mind, create possibilities, and assume the position not only in my mind and my heart but in my LIFE! Talk about the law of attraction! However, the most important aspect of manifestation is the FEELINGS you emit. This is why 'Act as If' events are essential. An 'Act as If Event' is when you go to a party dressed and acting like your future self! I changed the name to an 'Act Like You Know' event.

When you act like you know enough, then your body and mind begin to move towards that which you desire. Again, don't forget to truly feel and embody what you are acting. I have some questions I'd like to ask you.

- How would you act if you knew you couldn't fail? (I love this question!)
- What position would you assume in life?
- What would you create for yourself, your family, your life?
- Who would you be?
- How would you dress?
- How would you walk? (That was for Duke!)

- Where would you go?
- Where would you live? Be specific.
- Who would hang out with?
- Last question.

WHAT ARE YOU WAITING FOR?

Your Position Determines Your Ability to Swing

In racquetball, your position and your opponent's position determine the type of shot you can take and the level of power you administer. If I'm in the front and my opponent is in the back, then I will lightly tap the ball so it won't travel back to where my opponent can get to the ball quickly. Tapping the ball forces my opponent to get out of position.

However, if my opponent is at the front of the court, then I will hit the ball with more force, thus, driving the ball deeper to the back, far from their reach. If they are on the right side of the court in the front, then I'll hit a hard line drive down the left side of the court because I know they can't get to the ball fast enough. Let's say that my opponent is in the middle of the court, then I will hit a ceiling shot causing them to move back. This forces them to move out of position and allows me to move into the middle, which is the prime position, center court.

Being in PRIME position is key!

Being in the prime position allows you easy access to your goal. By no means am I telling you in life that you have to move someone out of position in order to succeed. I'm saying if your current position is not where you would like it to be, then you have to be willing to do something different in order to move into a prime position, THE CENTER COURT!

The Wrong Position

No matter where I seemed to move, I was out of position or did not get to the ball quick enough. At this point, my mind started to play tricks on me. Thoughts of defeat began to take over as Tracy called the score before serving. I stood in the middle so I could access both sides of the quite court. Being in the wrong position can be costly. For example, if I am standing on the right side of the court, I will have to use my backhand because I am left-handed. Although I can take a good swing, I am more powerful hitting a ball that is to my left, my strong side. Tracy is aware of my strengths and weaknesses which allows her to have an advantage over me when she is serving the ball.

When you notice that you are in the wrong position…

MOVE!

Reposition to Leverage Your Shot.

Many people may have started at the back of the court in life. Maybe they grew up in a dysfunctional setting where abuse, neglect, or abandonment was an everyday occurrence. Many of my virtual mentors have stories of adversity. Nevertheless, they seized opportunities that repositioned themselves from the back of the court to the front, from obscurity to triumph. Wayne Dyer, one of my favorite YouTube mentors, grew up in a foster home. He went from being abandoned to being accepted by millions! Oprah and her mentor Maya Angelou both experienced the trauma of being sexually assaulted. Yet, both went on to achieve acclaimed success as activists, voices of reason, and spiritual freedom.

My brother and I were raised by a single mother on welfare who only had a fifth-grade education, which limited her ability to find good jobs. All she thought she could do was be a maid in the suburbs of Philadelphia and clean houses. Every day she would take two buses and the subway leaving the inner city of rowhomes traveling to the suburbs of Chestnut Hill to clean a 7-bedroom, 7-bathroom baby-mansion. Our entire third-floor row home apartment which constituted a kitchen, a bathroom, a room my younger brother and I shared, my mother's bedroom which also served as our living room, all could fit in the living room of the baby mansion she cleaned.

Although my mother only had a 5th grade education, she wanted more for us. She stressed the importance of getting a good education. I am currently an educator and hold two degrees and currently working on my dissertation towards a doctorate in mathematics education. This is not to mention the numerous certificates and training I have received throughout my career. My point is not to boast, but to impress upon you, that no matter where you start in the game, you have the power to determine your position. Your thoughts will guide you on your journey to hitting the winning shots in your life.

Sometimes your opponent in life may not be a physical opponent, but your own thoughts telling you that you are not worthy enough to win in life. Worst, you see evidence that things seem to be working against you. You hear thoughts in your head that say, "you came from nothing", "who do you think you are going for your doctorate, starting your own business, wanting a better job or a promotion, wanting a new home", "you are not strong enough, wise enough, smart enough", "you are too tall, too short, too fat, too skinny, too dark, too light, too - whatever"!

Your opponent will always remind you of the shot you missed the last time you swung that racquet. It will remind you of the shot you never took. That opponent may say: "You failed at the marriage, failed your children." "You got fired from that job." "You're just not good enough." "You don't have enough money for that." "You're too old." "You're too young." Blah blah blah!

Your opponent is hitting the ball faster, harder, making you chase out-of-reach shots that impedes your dream of pursuing your dreams of success. These subconscious thoughts have you at an unfair disadvantage and all it takes is **one mindset-shift...**

"YES, I CAN!"

"YES, I WILL!"

"YOU JUST WATCH ME!"

This ONE shift can change your position on the court of life! The moment you say out loud or to yourself, *"I GOT THIS"*, no matter what the game looks like, you transition into a winning mental position. A mental position shift allows you to hit your best shot when opportunities become available. As a matter of fact, you don't have to wait for opportunities, you...

ATTRACT & CREATE OPPORTUNITIES!
1 point at a time!

The other day I was checking my PAYPAL account to contact a supplier for some items I had not yet received and noticed that there was $1,100 waiting for me from a previous course I created! It amazes me when I think about how I simply created a course from thoughts and got paid to help people. Zig Ziglar said, that *"If you help enough people get what they want, you will get what you want."*

My mentor, Bob Yates, would have us make declarations at the beginning of his workshops, and two of my favorites were:

"I CREATE MY OWN ECONOMY!" and

"MONEY FLOWS TO ME ABUNDANTLY!"

You have the ability, the power, and the tools within you, to create and design your desired destiny and play your game on your own terms! Only YOU have the power to change your position. You are where you are, but you don't have to stay there. Acknowledge where you are but keep moving forward. It starts with your mindset and knowing your position. It starts with knowing who you are and whose you are along with the gifts and talents YOU bring into the world.

At one of Bob's training, he told us a story from the bible (Mathew 25). Although I go to church, I'm not very good at quoting scripture, but I remember this one. This particular scripture is about a merchant who went out of town for business, leaving three servants to take care of things. He gave the first servant 5 talents of which he invested and doubled the talents. He gave the second 2 talents of which he doubled. He gave the third servant 1 talent of which he buried to keep it safe. When the merchant returned, he was pleased with the two servants who had multiplied the talents, he called them "Good and faithful servants". He put them both in charge of much more. When he was told that the third servant buried the talent, he was furious. In fact, he called him lazy and good for nothing.

What are you doing with your talents?

Are you ready to move to CENTER COURT?

Point 4
Your Mindset is Key,
Not the Score

Back Court - the area of the court between the short line and the back wall.

> "To be the champ you have to believe in yourself when nobody else will."
>
> *Sugar Ray Robinson*

Mindset-You Will Find That Which You Seek

The game is intense, the taste of salt from the sweat that trickled down the right side of my cheek entered the corner of my mouth. The score is 10-2 and I still can't believe I am losing by 8 points! Tracy is in the front doing her Barney Rubble victory dance because she had just made another point.

It's amazing how your thoughts impact how you play a game. You can have 10 and your opponent may have 2 and the person with 10 may think *"oh I got this"* and start to ease up. Or they may think: *"oh I got 10, I need to just go ahead and seal the deal!"* The person with 2 may *think "I might as well give up because I am too far behind and will never catch up, I'll get them in the next game."* On the other hand, the person with the 2 may think *"I can still win, the party ain't over, I can turn it around, I just need to take my time and focus on one point at a time, I'm going to give it my all!"* Your mindset serves as momentum to move you forward or it can stop you in your tracks causing you to throw in the towel. Reminding you of a time when you were not successful.

> *"Your past needs to remain in the past, if you bring your past to your present, then your past will be in your future."*
> Dineen Merriweather

This is not the time to let the frustration of a lower score control your thoughts. That's when you start making mistakes! If you are focusing only on the score, there is no way you can possibly catch up. The universe is always responding to your thoughts. It is the basic Law of Reflection. Our thoughts shape our reality. The moment you think you have lost, you're right and conversely, the moment you think you have won, you win. Growing up I would always hear the phrase 'winners always win, and losers always lose' it wasn't until recently that I truly understood that statement. Winners ALWAYS expect to win, and losers ALWAYS expect to lose.

What do you expect?

Our words HAVE POWER, they have energy!

There is power in the tongue.

Our words can heal or hurt, lift up or let down, develop or destroy, awaken or anchor, you get the picture. If you don't believe me, Google the rice experiment. In this experiment people have three containers of cooked rice. The first container the person would scream and shout at it saying mean and hurtful things like, I hate you! You are ugly, you are stupid, I wish you were dead. (Yup I know, this sounds weird, stay with me). They would then say loving things to the second container of rice. Things like, I love you. You are so beautiful. I am so happy I have you. And for the third container, they would simply ignore it. That's right, they would ignore the rice. (How can you ignore rice?) in other words, they did not talk to the container of rice. They would then set each container of rice on the shelf and repeat the daily verbal routine, screaming and yelling at the first container, saying loving words to the second container and ignoring the third. After a week you could see a difference in the appearance of rice in each container. You would see specks of mold in the first container that had been yelled at while the second container that had received only loving, kind words had no mold. Get this, the third container that was being ignored had more mold than the first container of rice! Each week you would see more mold on the first and third container while the second had little to no mold.

The rice experiment was a spinoff of Masaru Emoto's work. Emoto claims that our words or thoughts have dramatic effects on water. He claims that, depending on the words or thoughts directed at water, when frozen its crystals will be "beautiful" or "ugly" depending on whether the words or thoughts were positive or negative. If this is true, then words have dramatic implications on our bodies. It is a fact that 75 percent of all biological tissue, including the human body, is made up of water.

Our words and thoughts create changes to our bodies! Dr. Joe Dispenza talks about it extensively in his book' You Are the Placebo'. Our words and thoughts are potent!

> *"If you don't see yourself as a winner, then you cannot perform as a winner."*
> Zig Ziglar

There's a part in the Bible about a beggar who is sitting outside of a city and is approached by a traveler. The traveler asked the beggar, "*What will I find beyond the city walls?*" The beggar replied, "*You will find that which you seek.*" In other words, you will find whatever it is that you are looking for. If you are looking for 'good', you will find 'good'. However, if you're looking for 'bad', you will find 'bad'. Some people, no matter what they do, always see the bad. You know who these people are. I'm quite sure you can think of that person right now.

"When you change the way, you look at things, the things you look at, will change."
Wayne Dyer

Maybe you should share the above quote with them.

I think we've all experienced this in some way or another. We must be mindful of what we think about and try not to harbor the negative thoughts. I'm not saying not to think about anything negative, I'm just saying acknowledge them then move on past them. Let them go. I was talking to my friend Tonya who does extensive training clients in the 'Circle of Forgiveness'. Before she could train anyone on forgiveness, she had to go through the exercises herself. When Tonya completed her forgiveness cycle series, she was able to release the hurt and frustration and move beyond her circumstances. As a result of Tonya forgiving those people who hurt her, only then she was able to be free. During our conversation, Tonya shared how she had crossed the path of someone she had to forgive, and because she had a different perspective and had forgiven them, she was able to not be affected by that person's presence.

Thoughts create actions,

Actions create results,

Results create moments,

Moments determine success or failure.

It is a chain effect that starts with your thoughts.

What do you typically think about?

Do you have more positive thoughts or negative thoughts?

Are you busy focusing on someone else's score?

Don't Focus on Someone Else's Score

In this world of social media, it is easy to get distracted by the sensationalism of everyone's life. People seldom post ugly pictures of themselves on Facebook, Twitter, Instagram, TikTok, or the host of other social platforms. They only post pictures of the good times. They are celebrating weddings, but not divorces. They are celebrating the new house, but not the sacrifices they went through to get the new home. They post their children graduating from high school but not about the struggle it was to keep them jokers focused.

Too often, we focus on their score and forget that we are in a game ourselves. I was speaking to a friend who was saying she got back in the game when she heard her pastor give a sermon about being the spectator of a game instead of actually being a player in the game. She realized that she was watching the score of everyone else's game and not her own. It is easy to buy a ticket to watch someone else win or lose rather than actually getting out there to play the game ourselves. Don't be too focused on *'the watching'*. Some will pour all their resources on purchasing a ticket to watch a game, rather than invest it in their own growth, conditioning, and training to ensure they are in optimal condition to PLAY THEIR OWN GAME.

I have seen people pay hundreds of dollars to go to a sporting event, even thousands depending on the level of the sport, yet they will cringe at the price of having a coach who can help them get to their next level in life. It is not about being able to afford a coach, it is the mindset. One of my coaches Melissa would always say, "it's never the money, it's the mindset." Why do we find more value in that moment of cheering for someone else than investing in our own growth... repositioning our future or getting prepared?

Thank goodness that is not you. Even if you do not have a personal coach yet, you are currently reading this book. You are investing in your future, in your mind-shift, in getting primed, prepared, and positioned at center court to win.

Never Ever Base Your Ability on Someone Else's Thoughts or Actions

Never allow someone's action or inaction to determine how you play your game. Most people allow others to take control of the steering wheel. They turn on the cruise control and sit idling in the passenger seat being driven to a destination not of their choosing.

How? Why?

Somebody criticized their work, so they stopped writing. Somebody didn't show up for them the way they expected them to, so they quit and threw in the towel. Someone else has forty thousand YouTube followers and they only have 100 so they decide not to try. They're too busy looking at what their opponent is doing and not playing their own game. They assume the position of a victim which in turn, causes them to get stuck and not move forward towards their dreams, hopes, and aspirations of becoming a victor.

Sometimes it is our parents who might dictate our career. Or maybe you are the breadwinner in your household, and you are afraid to quit your job to pursue your dream because your family is depending on your income. Or maybe you spent years climbing the corporate ladder only to realize that the ladder you were climbing is against the wrong building.

You may need to make the necessary adjustments to get into and stay in the game of your choice. Keep track of your own score so that you will know you are headed towards your markers. You will have to remember to keep your head in the game. The mindset is key! This is where you will have to step up your game. Remember you are still in the game until the buzzer sounds, the last point is scored. You are not like most people who give up before the game is over. You got this! Seal the deal when you have

10! Play to win when you have only 2 points! Believe in yourself! Don't quit!

> *"The greatest achievement was at first and for a time a dream. The oak sleeps in the acorn; the bird sleeps in the egg; and in the highest vision of the soul, a waking angel stirs. Dreams are the seedlings of realities..."*
> *James Allen*

How do you plan to score?

How will you celebrate when you win this game?

Point 5
You Must Play with Grace and Ease

Drive - an aggressively hit, fast moving ball.

> *"When you are in harmony with yourself everything unfolds with grace and ease."*
> Panache Desai

Be Easy, it's gonna be ready when it's ready

I looked up synonyms for the word grace. Here is what I found: elegance, refinement, effortlessness, polish, beauty, style, poise, proficiency, simplicity, and dexterity. The more I thought about the score, the more anxious and unrefined I became. I was not polished at all, I kept missing the ball or if I connected with the ball, I would make an error. It seemed as if that day was not my day. I exhibited no style, poise nor proficiency!

I did however, noticed that there was a direct correlation between my anxiety and my errors. They both were on a rise and my opponent could tell. This reminds me of my dogs Sasha (Fierce) and Stewart (Little) whenever they would encounter a person who was frightened of dogs, they would be more aggressive. However, when they come across a person who was not afraid and wanted to pet them, my dogs would bark and simultaneously back away. Apparently, Tracy could sense my anxiety and she was out for blood! I on the other hand, could sense her position of confidence, and the only way this energy shift can change is if **I** make the shift.

When you are nervous or anxious, it's hard to be in flow or operate with grace and ease. When you are operating in grace and ease you are playing in your lane of genius, you are fluid, smooth with it, like a warm knife cutting through room temperature butter. Smooth like an expert swimmer doing laps, arms like blades fluidly slicing through the water, smooth! When you are calm, comfortable, and confident! Like a winner, you expect to win.

It is when you are playing with grace and ease, it's hard to be knocked off your 'A' game.

Be in Flow. Flow does not let someone get in your head. You get into your own head.

Just Breathe

Sometimes in life, you find yourself running so fast you can't seem to catch your breath! You're here, you're there, doing this, doing that, doing this, AND that! You are out there on your grind, sometimes chasing dreams that may not even be yours. You're so busy chasing your dreams that you're out of breath. You have to remember to catch your breath so as not to pass out. RELAX! In a relaxed state, you can think clearly and rationally. "Breathe DEEP" as my husband Chris would say. It is central, it slows down your heart rate, it calms your thinking and your anxiety. When you take a deep breath, it allows oxygen to go to your brain. Another important thing to remember about breathing is to expand your diaphragm. Breathing is key, research suggest that it changes your brain's chemistry. That's why meditation and breathing exercises are important.

Relax and Focus

Relaxation brings about focus and focus helps you get into a better position. When you're focused you know where you're going, and you may have an idea of how you're going to get there.

But when you are not relaxed you make abrupt moves and decisions. As a result, your swing may be too short, or you may overextend your reach, and nothing seems to work out.

In point 9, I talk about anticipating the ball and getting to the spot before the ball so I can make contact. I'm more relaxed because I know I can get there. Here is what I mean, if I anticipate where the ball is and get there, then I can relax knowing that I'm already in a position to make contact with the ball.

Don't rush it.

When was a time where you exhibited grace and ease?

_____
_____
_____
_____
_____
_____

Who would you have to be in order to show up with grace and ease?

_____
_____
_____
_____
_____
_____

How. Would it look for you to show up with grace and ease?

_____
_____
_____
_____
_____
_____

Point 6
Own YOUR Game

Ace – a serve that isn't returned, results in a point for the server.

"Start Where You Are. Use What You Have. Do What You Can."
Arthur Ashe

Social Noise

Jon Acuff said, "Don't compare your beginning to someone else's middle." In other words, don't compare your 2 years of experience to someone's 20 years of experience.

Quit comparing yourself to others! This point is key! We all have different skills, and different experiences that make up who we are, and how we navigate in the world. Too often we compare ourselves with others.

- We compared our homes
- We compared our cars
- We compared our clothes
- We compared our jobs
- We compared our children, our spouse,
- You name it, we compare it!

We don't realize what people had to go through in order to get where they are.

In 2014, Chris and I went to a coworker's party at his home. Mitch and his wife had a nice house in Upper Marlboro Maryland and an expensive sports car in the garage. They had three beautiful children, two boys, and a girl, and the house was full of their family and friends. From the outside looking in, it seemed as if they had all the trappings! When we left the party, we climbed into our blue 2008 Jeep Liberty and I said to Chris with admiration, "wow, Mitchell and Diane have everything, a beautiful home, a shiny sports car, three kids, a dog, and a cat!" Well maybe not a dog and a cat but you get the picture.

As we drove past rows of neatly manicured green lawns he said: "yeah, they have all that, but did you notice that Mitch and Diane never once interacted with each other?" I thought about that for a second and I realized I didn't see them talk to each other, not once the whole time we were there. I just thought they were busy entertaining their guests.

A year later, Mitch and Diane were divorced. It was then I realized that you can't judge peoples' lives and you shouldn't compare! You can't compare your life to other people because you don't really know what's happening behind closed doors. People only show you what they want you to see. Everyone has filters. Like I said before, people on Facebook and Instagram, only show the good stuff. They put on filters to hide their flaws and imperfections. You don't know their troubles, their trials of tribulations, you only see the facade. You only see the outside, the well-manicured green lawns. You only see what they're showing you. So don't compare, appreciate what you have, and work on improving yourself, not comparing. The only person you should be measuring yourself against is you. Be better than you were yesterday. You don't need to compete with anybody.

In other words,

STAY IN YOUR LANE!

Focus

I was so focused on how that ball hit the left corner so low that I could not return Tracy's shot! I was so busy admiring her shot when I was supposed to get ready to return the ball. As a result, I miss my shot because I was too busy celebrating her shot. In life, we're so busy looking at other people's shots that we forget to focus on our own shots. If you are not good at something, then study and become good at it or make it a hobby, not your career. Like Jim Rohn said, *"Don't spend MAJOR time on minor things."* **Spend major time on your passion**, the stuff that's already in your lane and your heart!

You need to focus on your own goals, your own aspirations, your own ideas, your own ventures. You can't be the Jack of all trades. (I'm still working on this part!) As a creative with ideation as one of my top strengths, I have all these great ideas. The problem comes when I try to implement them all at the same time! Find your niche and specialize in it.

People seek help from those who specialize in things not with someone who does a lot of different things. For example, if I need a heart surgeon, I'm not going to someone who is not a specialist. What about you, would you go to a non-specialist?

Stay in Your Lane

I have a coach who's helping me with my writing and although I do a lot of training and workshops, I realized that writing is something that I would have to get support in order to do well. In other words, writing is not my forte. At least, that was what I was told as a freshman in college. Just the other day I was listening to a course. This particular course was on how to write an eBook. I always heard that the best way to learn something is to teach it. So naturally, I thought, maybe I can teach people how to write an eBook.

I thought about how I would set it up. I thought about how much I would charge. I even thought about how long the course would be! My brain was taking me down a path of unfamiliar terrain. Then I thought, wait a minute, why would I want to create a course on writing an eBook that's not my lane. I realized that I can't be the jack-of-all-trades. I need to stick to what I do best, hone those skills, and then bring all my skills to that game! Gallup found that when people work on their weaknesses, they became competent, however, if they work on their strengths, then they became excellent!

Driving in My Lane

I've taught math for over 29 years. I taught high schoolers mathematics for fourteen of those years and trained teachers and administrators for the remaining 15 years. Last year I was helping one of the teachers with achieving National Boards Certification. This certification is very prestigious and allows teachers to teach anywhere in the United States. The teacher's background is secondary mathematics, and her original coach background was in Early Childhood education. So, it may not seem like it's a big difference, but it is. I specialize in secondary mathematics. I'm able to help the teachers see different nuances as it relates to high school mathematics but more importantly, how to teach it in such a way that makes sense. I'm not saying that her original coach is not able to support her, I am quite sure she is highly capable. I do know that coaching and supporting secondary teachers is my zone of genius. It's my lane. What's your lane?

Do You Boo!

Have you ever seen a plus size woman walking down the street just giving it! What I mean by giving it is, that she is confident! Hair done, fashionable clothes, makeup fierce, her head is high, and she is walking like she owns the world! You have to admire her! You can then see another plus size woman who may not have that same vote of confidence. You can tell the difference, even if she is dressed nice it's how she carries herself.

What I'm trying to say is embrace who you are. The way you walk, what you wear, how you choose to wear your hair. OWN IT! BOSS UP! If you are a geek like me, rock your geekiness, rock it hard. Love hard. Say to yourself, this is who I am. It is what it is and I am who I am. This is my game. Own all the good and the bad. And when you do and show up doing what you do best, then you will never have to chase the money, the money will start to chase you!!!!

Oftentimes stepping into your authentic self may be seen as you are being defiant. Like coach Dineen would say, "Who cares! Let them kick rocks with open toe shoes!"

Bring All of YOU to the Table

When I was working with my business coach Melissa, she had us complete us a quarterly assignment. In this assignment, we had to share our plans, projects, and programs for the next quarter. I had just come back from a four-day training with the John Maxwell Team. As a John Maxwell speaker and coach, I had a plethora of leadership materials. When I shared my assignment with all my programs and offerings, they were all John Maxwells. It was someone else's materials. I distinctly remember my coach asking me, "I understand that you are a member of the John Maxwell Team, but where are 'YOU' in these programs?" she was asking me where was my identity? It was then when I realized that I was nowhere in my future! I realize that I had to bring all of myself to the table and create my own products and services! Now when I create workshops, I bring out the poetic side, the athletic side, the quirky nerdy math puzzle-solving side to my unique equation.

So, my question for you is what are the variables in your unique equation?

I have a math problem to assist you at answering the above question.

> Pick a number between 0-9, then double your number, now add 2, now I want you to cut the total in half, finally, subtract your original number. What did you get? Now select a different number and do it again. Did you get the same number? Try any number. No matter what number you try, you will always get 1.

Question?

What makes you number 1 at that thing you do best?

___

What is that one thing that people come to you for help?

___

List those things below.

___

___

___

___

___

___

___

___

___

___

___

___

___

___

___

___

Remember, **PLAY YOUR GAME**, your contribution is needed.

And remember, it's BIGGER than you!

> *"It's your road and yours alone. Others may walk it with you, but no one can walk it for you."*
> **Rumi**

Point 7
Unless you Swing!

Forfeit - conceding a game to an opponent, whether voluntarily or involuntarily due to an absence.

Failure to Move - a player does not move away from the ball's path in order to give his or her opponent the opportunity to return a shot cross court or down the line.

Side-Out - losing the opportunity to serve the ball, and thus to score.

"You always miss 100% of the shots you don't take."
Michael Jordon

Why are you here?

You were placed on this earth to experience life and play full-out, whatever game you decide to play. The only person that can decide how you play, is you. Statistics show that most people don't begin at all, stopping before they get started. For example, my friend Regina teaches reading to 3rd graders in a nearby county. This was her 14th year in the classroom, and she was ready to make a change from teaching students to supporting teachers. She had been preparing for this move by serving as the department chair at her elementary school where she taught. Every week she would collaborate with Peggy, a literacy coach who had been assigned to her school. Peggy had been teaching and coaching for over 30 years and had taken Regina under her wings, grooming her to take over her position when she retired at the end of the school year.

The Self Sabotage

Every summer Regina would open her home to other teachers so they could prepare for the upcoming year. At the end of the year, Peggy retired, and her position was filled by one of the teachers Regina invited to her home for her annual summer preparation. Unfortunately, Regina did not apply for the coaching position although she was well qualified. I'm not sure if Regina learned the lesson. But I did. I learned to give it a go.

Swing. At least try.

You cannot get discouraged before you get started. Change

is uncomfortable, except for a wet baby. Stepping outside of our comfort zone can be scary and challenging. If you want to create something different, you have to do something different. I love this quote by Wayne Dyer, *"Progress is impossible if you always do things the way you've always done things."*

I was facilitating my Level Up Bootcamp and I had the participants create a bullseye. Inside the bullseye, they recorded all the things they were doing or wanted to do. The most comfortable things were closer to the center and the least comfortable things were closer to the edge of their bullseye.

They were then asked to put some things they wanted to do but were not comfortable doing on the outer edge of the bullseye. They each selected one new thing that was out of their comfort zone they would like to try. Each person agreed to give it a go and within three to four weeks they each expanded their comfort zone! Francine started her Instagram account, Linda said 'no' unapologetically, Diane started coaching a small group of women and Juanita said yes to an opportunity she would not have said yes to in the past and ended up on television! In other words, they stepped outside the boundaries and stepped over that red line and created a new comfort zone!

Then you have people that will try something once, fail once only to never try again. Saying things like, "I've tried that before and it didn't work for me." "I'm like my father, I don't like to sell." Those who are successful are those who have failed and failed again. People like Abraham Lincoln, Walt Disney, Steven

King, Oprah Winfrey, JK Rowling, Bill Gates, Colonel Sanders, and Michael Jordan. They kept trying despite their failures, loss, and defeat, they persevered. Because they took a swing and kept swinging, and kept swinging, and kept swinging, you get the picture. They eventually became successful.

Dust it Off!

In February, just before the pandemic, I went to Honduras with Tracy to hang out with her daughter who was working there. I had such a delightful time backpacking across the countryside. We went white-water rafting, hiking we visited a natural hot spring we had a ball! We stayed at several Hostels throughout the countryside. I had everything for my two weeks stay in a backpack. Just 4 months later I was doing laundry when I found the backpack in the closet on the floor and inside the backpack was some of my favorite comfortable outfits that I totally forgot about.

Sometimes when things are out of sight they tend to be out of mind as well. What are some things that you've tried before and have not had success and you put it aside dismissing your efforts? I invite you to look in the closet of your brain, on the top shelf way in the back. Go ahead, pull it out and blow the dust off those ideas. Take out of the box, or backpack and begin to play with those ideas again. Maybe you can figure out what went awry.

When I was in the Army, we used to do AAR's or After-Action Reviews. After an exercise or a mission, we would debrief to unpack those things that went well and how we might continue those things in future missions. Then we would discuss those things that did not go so well and ways in which we might do something different to get better results the next time. That's what successful people do, they analyze, they celebrate all the things that went well and then they analyze those things that didn't go so well and readjust for success.

Dust it off!
Go ahead, take a swing!
One point at a time!
Then focus on the next step.
Visualize the next point!

Next thing you know you're gaining momentum!
The only way you're getting there is because you keep swinging!
No one will know how GREAT you could be, not even you.

SWING!

What would you do if you knew you would ace whatever you would swing at? What would be that thing you would try?

_____
_____
_____
_____
_____
_____

What are five things you can do to move you closer to winning?

_____
_____
_____
_____
_____
_____

Which one would you like to try first?

_____
_____
_____
_____
_____
_____
_____

Point 8
Reach for it!

Safety Zone - the region of the court between the short line and the receiving line; the receiver is prohibited from entering this area during the serve.

> *"Everything is energy and that's all there is to it.*
> *Match the frequency of the reality you want,*
> *and you cannot help but get that reality.*
> *It can be no other way.*
> *This is not philosophy.*
> *This is physics."*
> ~ Albert Einstein

Reach

Here we are in the middle of a rally, Tracy hits a ball to the opposite side of the court! As I stare at the ball, my mind is saying *"there is no way I can get that ball"* but my body was already in motion! Before I knew it, I was sending a line drive for a kill shot to the lower-left corner! That was the shot that turned the game around! Tracy didn't think that I would be able to return that ball. Heck, I didn't think I was going to be able to return the ball! You get what you go for!

> Strength doesn't come from what you can do. Strength comes from overcoming the things you once thought you couldn't.
> Unknown

What is that one thing that you need to do that will turn the game around?

We all know what that one thing is. It's typically that one thing that we've been hesitant about doing but if we were to do it. It could be the game-changer! For instance, do you need to take a course that you've been putting off? Maybe take that math class that you've been avoiding. Learn how to speak in public or learn how to invest in the stock market or trade currency in the foreign exchange market. What's that one thing that you may need to take a swing at that might be life-changing for you and your family?

The 'F' Word

Don't listen to that negative mind chatter and allow the ball to pass you by. The score would have been 12 - 2! Oftentimes, it's the negative mind chatter that paralyzes us causing us not to lung forward and reach for our goals. My friend Shinika, who is an entrepreneur, said: It is a guaranteed NO if you don't make the call." That four-letter 'F' word stops many people dead in their tracks!

FEAR!

False

Evidence

Appearing

Real

Which causes us to **Forget Everything and Run!** We were born with just two fears, the fear of falling and the fear of loud noises, the rest, we were taught. Fear limits your potential. The longer we sit in the gap of fear the bigger the fear gets, then five years from now we see someone living our dream. In his book, John Maxwell talks about 5 fears that cause people not to move forward: the fear of failure, trading security for the unknown, being overextended financially, what others would say or think, that success will alienate peers. I'd like to add another. The fear of leaving this earth without playing your game full out and experiencing life to its greatest potential. In order for you to be able to play full out and win you have to invest in your highest commodity…

YOU!

My job became my financier! I had to budget and invest in my future if I wanted to design my desired destiny and live my life in 3D. I no longer wasted money on things that I perceived as a low ROI, I invested in personal development, participated in masterminds, watched YouTube's, took online, and face to face courses, hired coaches, heck I even became a coach! I became a John Maxwell speaker and coach, a Clifton Strength Finders coach, I took Danielle Leslie's course (on how to create a course), Dineen Merriweather, Melissa Hughes, Ted McGrath course, a slew of Udemy courses just to name a few.

I took notes after notes after notes. I became a professional note-taker! However, there comes a time when I need to put all that theoretical rigamarole into practice and just DO the doggone thing! It is an easy principle but may not be as easy to apply. It's one thing to reach within your ability, but it's another to reach beyond where you're already capable of reaching.

R E A C H!

Which fear might be holding you back?
Highlight the ones that has got you stuck.
Remember: You have to first acknowledge that thing that has you stuck before you can move past it.
F.E.A.R. has three meanings:

False Evidence Appearing Real

Forget Everything and Run

or

Face Everything and Rise.

The choice is yours and YOURS ALONE.

More Questions
- What are you listening to?
- What do you put inside your brain?
- What are you listening to when you're driving to work?
- What or who are you listening to when you're sitting around during lunch?
- What do you talk to your friends about?
- Is the conversation congruent with your goals?
- If not, what can you do to turn the game around?
- How are you trusting your intuition?
- How are you spending your time?
- Do you spend time, waste time, or invest time?
- When is it your time?
- What must you remove from your plate in order to make time to pursue your dreams?
- Who can you invite into the game to help you sharpen your skills?

What time is it for you?

Is it time to:
- Write your book and/or a blog?

- What would you write about?
- What inspires you?
- Work on your business plan?
- Will you be a sole proprietor, or will you have business partners?
- Start your YouTube channel, podcast?
- Create a course?
- What are you really good at doing?

It's time to plan out what you are trying to manifest for your future! It's time to make contact with those people who you can collaborate with to help you to move forward. Remember, no matter how slow you go, forward is forward!

Reach beyond your capacity.

Reach for it!

If your ship doesn't come in, SWIM OUT TO MEET IT!
Jonathan Winters

Point 9
Go Where the Ball is Going

"Knowing where you are going is the first step to getting there"
Ken Blanchard

Anticipate, Get there, Swing!

You have to be open to meet opportunity, then beat it to its destination! In other words, go where the ball is going! To be successful you can't go where the ball has already been, by that time it will be too late to swing. You have to anticipate where the ball is going and then beat the ball to the location in order to make the connection! How does this relate to your world?

Anticipate!

Knowing the patterns of how the ball reacts to the back wall, side walls, corners and ceiling is key at projecting where the ball may fall. Like many sports, angles play an important part in the movement and trajectory of the ball. When I first started playing racquetball, it was hard to predict or anticipate the movement of the ball, however, the more I played the game the more I became aware of the bouncing characteristics of the small pink ball. Each colored ball had a different bouncing pattern. The blue and green balls are the slowest to react whereas the pink and the red balls have a faster bouncing pattern which gives you less time to react.

Think about where you are trying to go in life.

Are you going after the blue ball that has a slower pattern which will allow you to have ample time for you to get into position? Or, are you going after the red or the pink ball which has a quicker bouncing pattern which means that you must have a quicker response rate? Regardless, you have to know the pattern of the bounce of the ball you are playing with before you can get there before the ball gets there. That means you have to study each ball bouncing pattern.

Where are you trying to go? What patterns do you need to observe? Who can you watch and learn from? What are you trying to reach and how can you position yourself to meet your dream? In other words, what are the things you need to do to prepare yourself to get to where you want to go? Seek help to figure it out, then...

GET THERE!

Get There!

Once you have an idea of where you want to go and the things you need to do to prepare, you will have to make a plan or create a blueprint to map out your course of action to get you there. Some questions you may want to consider:

- Where exactly is there?
- Who can help me get there?
- Who is already there?
- What classes might I take to set me on the tract to get there?
- What certifications are needed to move me closer to there?
- Which coach or mentor is best suited to help me get there?

Many people create vision boards to help them begin to manifest their dreams into reality. Every year I create a vision journal to help me to map out what I want to create for the year as I work toward my three, five, and ten-year goals. I would carry my vision journal everywhere I would go, capturing notes, dreams, and ideas. This very book was outlined in my 'Speak up' section in my 2019 journal!

On the inside cover of each journal, I would use black markers to depict my current situation of traveling from school to school supporting mathematics teachers at various high schools in Prince George's County. On the adjoining page, I use colored pencils and markers to map out my desired destiny by delineating and envisioning what I wanted to create for myself. In 2017 I created my first vision journal because I got tired of having several different journals and trying to remember which journal had what information became frustrating.

When I first mapped out my desired destiny, I had everything including the kitchen sink on that page! But there were always two images I had in the first vision journal and the years that followed. Each year I would sketch a picture of me traveling the world, and a picture of me and my team speaking to audiences, providing training and workshops. With each year I had less on that page, my dreams became more clear, more vivid, and more focused! Like Leo Babauta said: *"Your focus determines your reality."* I soon began speaking to audiences and conducting training and workshops around the world! I manifested my dreams!

In 2001 while teaching mathematics at Northwestern High school, I misplaced my house and car keys. I went to the security office to file a report. After filling out the report, I rushed back to teach my third period algebra class. Following class, I called the security office and spoke to Mr. Martin. Mr. Martin, the lead investigator at the school was a tall handsome man in his early sixties, "Did anyone turn in my keys?" I asked. He replied: "No, not yet". Before hanging up the phone, I asked Mr. Martin the name of the other investigator, he said the name Christopher Watkins. Mr. Watkins was 6'3" slim built weighing about 205 pounds and was really handsome. I remember sitting towards the back of my classroom at my desk smiling as I wrote *Mrs. Christopher Watkins* in cursive at the bottom of my desktop calendar. You see, I even manifested my husband! Later, I found my keys in the classroom. To this day, Chris still thinks it was a ploy to trap him.

I was visualizing and manifesting way back then! Now I am more intentional about what I want to create for my life. The first time I created the vision journal, I drew a picture of me at a computer doing a class or webinar with thirteen monitors to represent each student or client. Two weeks later Vic from the Institute for Learning who I had not spoken to since she provided training for our county in 2006 reached out to me to see if I would teach an eight-week online course. She also wanted me to travel to Connecticut and provide training for a school district!

My vision came into fruition just two weeks after I drew it!

But that's not the kicker! When I received my roster for the online course, and I was amazed at what I saw! There were exactly thirteen students on the roster! The same number of computers I drew in my vision journal! I was astonished at how fast my vision manifested! Every year I have a *"Design Your Desired Destiny"* workshop to help people manifest the life they deserve.

What vision do you plan to manifest? Remember, your thoughts create your reality!

ALREADY BE IN POSITION TO STRIKE!

What are four points you took from this point?

_____

_____

_____

_____

_____

_____

_____

What is one thing you would like to create in your life?

_____

_____

_____

_____

_____

_____

What is one thing you plan to try?

_____

_____

_____

_____

_____

_____

_____

Point 10

Action Speaks Louder Than Words
Don't Talk Trash

Stroke Interference – a player moves or does not move in a way that prevents the opponent from taking a full swing when attempting to return the ball.

Screen – a rebounding ball that comes too close to the now defender, preventing the opponent from a fair chance to return the ball either because of limited physical space or visibility, this can be a fault serve.

Hinder – a situation that requires a replay because of interference or obstructed view.

> *A person's actions will tell you everything you need to know.*
> *Anonymous*

Trash Talkers Always Talking Loud, Ain't Saying Nothing!

I don't enjoy playing with an opponent who is always talking trash! Some people, I don't care what it is, they could be watching a game or playing a game, win or lose they're always talking trash! However, you have some people who talk the most trash when they are winning, but as soon as they begin to lose, all you hear are crickets, nothing, nadda! They have nothing to say. This is when you turn it up and dig deeper to make them eat their own words! I mean every last syllable, noun, and pronoun!

Mostly, these trash talkers are the ones who are telling you the things that you can't do. I've noticed that these trash talkers' purpose is to get you off of your game and bring about fear and intimidation. They want you to lose focus. Sometimes it is a ploy so they can muster up some confidence, but remember, it's false. If you are an astute player, like I know you are, then you will see right through their futile attempts to derail your success!

Oftentimes, when they see that you are not affected by their scheme, their plot backfires, leaving them licking their wounds. Sometimes these trash talkers aren't even in the game, they're sitting on the sidelines, in the stands, on the bleachers, outside the court, criticizing you and your game. You can always spot them because they are always criticizing something or someone. They shout and tell you what you should be doing and who you should be.

There is a name for them. We call them TROLLS, HECKLERS or SPECTATORS. When you are on the court playing your game, you have a different perspective from the spectators who are sitting on the sidelines, outside the court, or in the nosebleed section.

You have a close-up view because you are on the court, in the game. Don't listen to the spectators.

Spectators oftentimes are disguised as a friend, a coworker, maybe even a family member. You can't allow the spectators to throw you off your game! I repeat you CAN NOT allow the spectators to throw you off your game. Deep down inside you know what you want. If it was meant for them to do what you're doing, then God would have given them the dream. He gave it to you. Now, if you choose not to use it, then, that's your choice.

Trust your instincts and intuition. Put the spectators in the nosebleed section so when they're shouting, you can't hear what they're talking about. Why waste your time and energy engaging in conversations with people who don't know the rules to your game.

"Stop sharing your million-dollar ideas with 100-dollar people"
Steve Harvey

Finally, don't be like the trash talkers, let your actions speak for you! Let your walk speak louder than your talk.

Self-Sabotage 2.0

What if YOU are the one who is talking trash to you? What if it were you who was spreading doubt, poisoning your thoughts, and stifling your actions. Research shows that people who tear themselves down experience setbacks more frequently. I've been there. I said things to myself that I would not say to another human being. I've said things like:

I'm too old.

I'm too fat.

I have no hair.

I'm not enough.

I don't speak proper English.

I'll get found out.

I'm too far behind.

I'm dumb.

Blah, blah, blah.

I told myself things that made me feel less than unworthy. If this is something you may have done, then I invite you to start your day off with some positive affirmations or thoughts. Check out the Hit List in the back of this book to give you a jump start.

What are four points you took from this point?

_____
_____
_____
_____
_____
_____
_____

What is one thing you would like to change in your life?

_____
_____
_____
_____
_____

What is one thing you plan to try?

_____
_____
_____
_____
_____

Point 11
Make Adjustments

Because Sometimes You Take a Hit
But YOU Gotta Get Back in the Game

Avoidable Hinderance - a preventable and sometimes intentional movement to prevent an opponent from returning the ball, resulting in a loss of rally for the offending player.

"It's not whether you get knocked down, it's whether you get up."

Vince Lombardi

It's Gonna Hurt

Being hit with a racquetball is not fun at all! That little pink ball stings! Imagine you are facing the front of the court waiting to return the ball and all of a sudden... Smack! A ball traveling at 105 miles per hour or faster, hits you in the back! To make matters worse, a wet shirt from your sweat causes the ball to sting even more!

At some point, you may be behind in bills, lose a contract or a big client, need to purchase new equipment and your account is 'in the negative'. Sometimes in life when you're playing full-out you are going to take a hit and it's going to hurt and may even set you back. When this happens and it will, you have to lick your wounds and get back into the game and start swinging.

Your mind is telling you "I think I've had just about enough!" then you realize that the game is not over, nope 'The Party Ain't Over' in fact, you are just getting started. Ralph Waldo Emerson said: "Our greatest glory is not in never failing, but in rising up every time we fail." Don't give up, hold on tight!

Many businesses went under due to the COVID virus that has impacted the world. However, there were many businesses that thrived. Delivery services like Amazon, liquor and wine stores, meal prep delivery services and game makers just to name a few. I had to pivot and make adjustments myself. Although I had been doing most of my trainings online, I still had to revamp most of my face-to-face play shops. It was challenging at first but doable. You eagerly find solutions for the things you love.

For the Love of it!

The reason why you play the game in the first place is that you enjoy it, and you realize that oftentimes you will get hit but you still have to get back into the game because you LOVE THE SPORT OF IT! That's why it is key to do the things that EXCITE, INSPIRE, AND MOVE YOU! Because if you do not enjoy the game, it will be easy to give up.

The excitement of winning causes you to forget the pain. You forget about your sore muscles. You forget about the stinging sensation on your back that is going to leave a circular purple bruise from being hit by the ball. You forget about all those things because you are in the throes of the game, the excitement of the game, running back, and forth, diving for the ball, and returning a shot not allowing your opponent to get not one extra point!

Tell the truth, you love the late-night hours creating, designing, reaching goals, setting new goals, jumping over obstacles, collaborating with your team, overcoming the challenges, bouncing ideas off a critical ear, and making money moves! These are the things that excite you the most!

The thought of victories erases your memory of the challenges. You are excited about the possibilities of getting that new client or meeting new people, maybe even meeting a new business partner, hiring an assistant to help you! Maybe you are a coach who is excited about helping your clients to open new doors and opportunities that might move them closer to their goals! I love it when I am able to help my clients reach their goals! You forget the pain because you are DOING WHAT YOU LOVE MOST! You're in the game! Win or lose!

Sometimes you have to make early sacrifices so that you can win in the end. Remember, there are always going to be ups and downs, but you have to get back on your horse, start swinging, get back up, GET BACK IN THE GAME! You have to bounce back like that Bozo Bop bag doll that no matter how hard it gets punched; it springs back up ready for action!

What are some ways you can pivot or make an adjustment?

_____
_____
_____
_____
_____
_____
_____

What is one pivot that will set you moving in the right direction?

_____
_____
_____
_____
_____
_____
_____

How will you prepare to pivot?

_____
_____
_____
_____
_____
_____
_____

Point 12
Enjoy the Game

Alley - the area along the court's side walls, a down the line shot.

> "So often we become so focused on the finish line
> that we fail to enjoy the journey."
> Dieter F. Uchtdorf

Have fun! Give it a Go!

One thing for sure is that I really enjoy playing racquetball, it's a great form of exercise! Win or lose, it's just fun! The reason why I like racquetball is that it is a competitive sport. Unlike step aerobics or jogging on a treadmill or running around a track, racquetball involves skills, agility, speed, thinking, awareness, control, and placement of the ball! It is very strategic! Strategic is one of my top 10 strengths. Oh, by the way, I have nothing against step aerobics or jogging on a treadmill, I just know it's not for me.

It involves you not necessarily out-running your opponent but **out-thinking** them. This is why I enjoy the game so much! With any game, business, relationship, or a job, you should enjoy what you do. It's nothing more frustrating than to have to do something day-in and day-out that you don't enjoy.

Research shows that over 80% of Americans work at a job they hate! I can't begin to imagine going to a job or playing a game that I don't enjoy. It doesn't make sense, why play the game if you're not there to enjoy yourself and have fun?

How might you feel when you wake up and you're not excited about going somewhere or doing something. It's a downer, right? You're grumpy, you're dragging along, and your energy is low like a cell phone with only 1 bar of energy. You show up late because you don't want to be there. Imagine owning a business and your employees hate coming to work. Employee turnover and absenteeism will be high, costing you lots of money. On the other hand, how might you feel when you get up in the morning knowing that you're about to go do something that you absolutely love!

How might that affect your business if your employees love coming to work? People would stay late, work overtime to finish a job. They would go above and beyond and do their best! You got it! Happy employees = Serving more people = Greater Potential for Profit! As a Strength Finders coach, I enjoy helping teams leverage their strengths and creating a more productive and enjoyable work environment.

What do you love doing? How might you monetize it? **Press PAUSE and think about that before moving on.**

NOW, act as if you are doing that thing that makes you happy.

I mean Really THINK about it. **FEEL IT!**

I bet you're smiling, right now. You should be! Think about those things that excite you as soon as you wake up first thing in the morning and then at night, just before you go to sleep. Check out the 6-phase meditation read by Vishen Lakhiani; it is perfect at helping you think about what you want to create in your life.

> "Just play. Have fun. Enjoy the game."
> *Michael Jordan*

Trust the Process

You have to trust the process as with any sport, there are

times where you are going to be winning, and times when you are going to be losing. Although my opponent was ahead of me and I was behind, I knew that if I took one point at a time, I would eventually increase my score. So, therefore, I knew that I had to trust the process! I had to stay focused, relax, breathe, and play with grace and ease. I had to implement all the things in the previous points and play my game now!

Reflection is the key to getting better. You can't improve if you don't take the time to reflect on what you did well and then reflect upon the things that didn't go as well. You have people who try something once, fail and then throw in the towel. They never take the time to reflect on what went well and what didn't go so well. Always reflect and then try it again making the necessary adjustments. I once heard Tony Robbins say it's always good to fail forward. What that means is when you fail at least you are one step closer to success. The next time you try it, you will know what to avoid and how to fix or tweak what didn't go so well the first time. And if you should fail again, rinse and repeat and always fail forward.

> "Go for it! Let nothing stop you, do what you love, follow your heart...It's time you realize just how amazingly awesome you are!"
> Babz

And if you ain't enjoying the game anymore, then it's time for you to play a new game.

What are some things you enjoy most about the game you currently play?

Point 13
Next Level Up!

Rating - an evaluation of players' ability levels, based on their success versus local opponents.

The mediocre mentor tells. The good mentor explains.
The superior mentor demonstrates. The greatest mentors inspire!
Lucia Ballas Traynor

"No, I'm Good"

Have you ever offered someone something and you knew they needed what you were offering, only to have them reply, "no, I'm good" Is it that they are afraid of the unknown, or they are satisfied with their current status? Either way, it's their decision. I used to get frustrated, but I realize, they have the power to choose. Remember, you can not want something more for someone than they want for themselves.

I remember when I went to Bali for a retreat with my coach Melissa. We stayed in a beautiful villa; it was an oasis in the heart of Ubud! There was a private 40-foot lap pool and we each had our own suite. We were served breakfast, lunch, and dinner, prepared by authentic chefs! We even had a private gym on the property. A Masseuse came in and gave us the most amazing massage ever! We thought we had died and gone to heaven! So, you can imagine when our coach told us to pack our bags and that it was time to move on to the next place, needless to say, we didn't want to go. I mean can you blame us? We were living in the lap of luxury! We reluctantly packed our bags, and our party of seven loaded into the eight-passenger van parked outside the villa.

We were on the road for at least two hours travelling through the cities and across the countryside of Bali, passing people riding motorcycles to and from their destinations. We even saw a family of five on one motorcycle! The vehicle finally began to slow down. We had come to a valley or some sort of raven, it looked like a work zone or quarry. I thought we were lost at this point. We all looked at each other and thought to ourselves, "Why did we have to leave paradise?"

As we looked around there was no vegetation, it was just clay walls on both sides of the van. We thought Melissa had lost her everlasting mind! As our van turned the corner, the 14-foot-high clay walls were replaced by lush green vegetation, colors of pink, orange and yellow flowers lined the walls of the compound! Our vehicle pulled up to a beautiful villa in Pandawa! We walked across a little bridge and on both sides of the bridge was a little pond filled with koi fish and pink and white-water lilies! This new place not only had a private pool but two private pools! One on the lower level and another pool directly above it overlooking the ocean! The views were breathtaking! We each had our own rooms! The large private gym was surrounded by beautiful vegetation! The new place had all the amenities and more! And to think we didn't want to leave the other villa! Sometimes we're so used to 'good' that we close off the possibility of great! Mic Drop!

To play up sometimes means you have to leave the good. However, you must have an idea of what you want, then make a request to the universe. Get clear about what you desire at your next level, then ask for it knowing that it is already yours. Expect it! As Melissa would say "this or something better!"

What might better look like for you?

Play with Better Players

If you are trying to get better, you have to play up. That is, play with better players. Did you know that your salary is the average of your five closest friends? You've heard these saying before:

"Birds of a feather flock together."

"Show me your friends and I can tell a lot about you."

When you play with players who you know you will always beat, you only improve your ego! Playing with the least experienced players will give you the opportunity to focus on perfecting your skills. However, if you want to get really good at the game then you must play with more experienced players! You can't be afraid to play with champions! You cannot be insecure when playing with a champion you have to go all out or go home! It is when you are playing with an experienced player that you see shots that an inexperienced player isn't able to execute. Therefore, play with those people who are where you are trying go. Ms. Ruth told me one day after one of my trainings that you should hang out with people who has your solution and not your problems.

Play with different people that has your solution. You can't play with the same person and expect to have a variety of strategies. However, I just want to tell you, there are three types of players, the players that:

- TEACH you,
- INSPIRE you, or
- DETER you.

I'm going to give you an example of the three players, and I want you to tell me which one you think I'm talking about. I used to play racquetball with Jose, a co-worker who taught Spanish at

Northwestern High School. When we first started playing, we played at the same level but as the years progressed, he began playing with different and more experienced players oftentimes losing 15 to 0. As a result, Jose's game drastically improved, because he learned from better players! He was able to monopolize the court whenever we would play. As a matter of fact, he got so good he would take his time and show me some things he had learned. You guessed it; Jose taught me. ` It was a great investment of my time.

Think of a time when you learned something from someone that positively impacted your life. How did you grow as a result of that interaction? Maybe you are the one who is impacting others.

Another time, I remember playing with an old man, he had to be in his late sixties or early seventies. His name was Henry. I thought to myself. "Henry is going to be an easy target," I remember watching him play other players, seeing him hobble back and forth trying to retrieve the ball. I had speed and youth on my side. This old man who could barely move had me running all around the court chasing that little pink ball. I felt like a chicken with its head cut off running around the court chasing the ball. He knew exactly how to hit the ball so that I was unable to return it.

I was inspired by his ability to place the ball just beyond my reach. I learned that day that is not about speed or agility it was more about precision, strategy, and ball placement. It was a great way to spend my time. Who are some people who may have inspired you? write them a handwritten note thanking them. Then mail it off. Do not shoot them a text. It will make their day getting a handwritten thank you note in the mail, out of the blue!

Then there was this muscular guy I played. I've seen him play before with some guys several times. He was clearly a better player. When I asked him to play, he said yes however his game said no. He kept hitting the ball as hard and as fast as he could which did not allow me any opportunities to return the ball. I don't think I hit the ball once the entire game! Actually, it wasn't a game at all. The score was 15 to 0. I don't think he really wanted to play, he only wanted to dominate the court and humiliate me. It felt like he just wanted to get me off the court. He gave me no pointers whatsoever. He did not inspire or teach, he deterred. It was a total waste of my time. What has deterred you from doing what you want?

I learned from the muscular guy that there are people who dominate the game and don't believe in helping others learn. From the older guy, I learned you have to be patient, and strategic. But Jose taught me the most important thing. Play with different and better players. If you play with the same person all the time you only become accustomed to the way that person plays. You will never learn anything new. However, when you play with different people, you learn different techniques and strategies. When you have multiple strategies and skills, you have more OPPORTUNITIES and VERSATILITY!

Big people make you feel bigger, while small people make

you feel smaller. Run with the GIANTS, play with people you can learn from. Whenever I play with a more experienced player, I'm watching the shots they're making. I'm watching the placement of the ball. I watch how they hit certain shots forcing me to move out of position. I examine how they hold their racquet when they hit a particular shot. I would not be able to analyze the game unless I was in the game. In other words, you have to be in action!

Who or what has inspired you to take action?

You heard the saying before, you can't learn if you are the smartest person in the room. One thing that I do recognize is that when I play with better players it causes me to up my game. In other words, I PLAY BETTER. Time well spent!

How do you use your time? You can waste time, spend time, or invest time. The GREAT thing about this is, YOU GET TO CHOOSE.

Learn From an Expert Who is Familiar with the Terrain.

I went on a ski trip to Massanutten with my family and some good friends. There were five couples along with their families, Tracy and her husband was one of the five families who joined us. We had been skiing for two hours and the slopes were a little icy. Just as I was getting my rhythm Tracy's daughter, Brea recommended that we try a different slope. I figured that I was ready to give it a go. So, Brea, Carol (who just learned how to ski) and I jumped on the ski lift.

I saw skiers, and snowboarders descend down the icy-snow-covered slopes while we talked as the ski lift took us up the mountainside. Then without warning, Brea said "get ready to jump off now." "NOW!?" I replied. Brea looks across Carol who is sitting between us and said "Yes, if we don't get off now then this will take us to the next level, the diamond level". The diamond level is for expert skiers, of which I am not! It was either jump now or jump at a much higher altitude. I thought to myself, "I'll take my chances here" so I adjusted my body and scooted to the edge of the ski lift as we approached the landing.

As soon as we jumped off the ski lift the hill went straight down, I mean there was no space or time to prepare to go down the hill! As Carol and Brea went flying down the hill. I just knew this was the end of Carol! Like I said, she just learned how to ski! I noticed a wooden light pole and aimed my skis towards it and held on for dear life! I must have been there for 20 minutes, clinging to that light pole, trying to figure out how I was going to navigate down this unfamiliar icy terrain.

Both Brea and even Carol made it safely down the hill. Twenty-five minutes later, Brea emerged from the ski lift and patiently coaxed me down the mountain side until I got to the part of the slopes that was familiar. Thanks to Brea, I got to the bottom of the mountain in one piece!

I needed the help of someone who had been down that side of the mountain before, someone who was familiar with the terrain. You may need to hire a professional to save you time, energy, mistakes, and money.

Getting a mentor or a coach can help you navigate the terrain they have already traveled. Everyone learns from mistakes and there's no rule that states the mistakes have to be yours. Like I said earlier, *"A smart man learns from their mistakes, but a wise man learns from the mistakes of others"*. An experienced player or mentor can show you things that you haven't thought about that can assist you at taking your game to a new level.

They're Watching You

In 2018, I was at a speaking event. I could tell the guest speaker was very knowledgeable. The questions she asked really engaged the crowd, however, I had a hard time focusing on her words because her appearance wasn't congruent to her message. Her notes were a pile of crumpled papers, her hair was not very neat, and her dress was wrinkled. She looked like she had thrown on an outfit to run to the corner store. Now you may think that I may sound a little petty, however as a guest speaker or presenter you need to think about these things. Unfortunately, we do judge books by their cover. People are always watching not only what you do but HOW you do it.

I think that if she were standing in front of her executive clients, she would have dressed more appropriately but because she did not show up professionally for our group that made me wonder how she perceived us. Were we not good enough for her to dress her best? Don't get me wrong, I'm not saying that you should look impeccable, but what message are you sending to your audience when you don't fully show up or play up? You ARE your brand.

She showed me what NOT to do!

Played Up!

The following year, I attended a 3-day conference in New York City. The presenter of the conference came out in an elegant gown! Her hair was neat, I mean she looked amazing! She was calm and poised as she navigated her color-coded PowerPoint presentation, and she had a well-organized team! After she would present a segment her team, dressed in matching t-shirts, would spring into action, and pass out the color coded handouts that matched the PowerPoint. Each module was labeled and appeared to be coherent and sequential. More important, the information she shared was on point. The presentation and the conference were very professional and well thought out. She represented her brand well! Her packages were well delineated. She was very organized, and you knew what you were getting if you decided to purchase her services. What I really liked about the conference was she gave us an opportunity to reflect upon what we had learned.

Now THAT'S how you do it!

She showed me what to do!

You only have one chance to make a FIRST impression. We learn from everyone. The good and the bad.

What will your impression be?

What is your brand?

The Next Level!

This is why you need a coach or a mentor to guide you. The life coaching industry is increasing drastically! People are looking for help from people who have already walked the walk and are actually in the game doing the stuff! More importantly, you have to be opened to listen and learn. An old Turkish proverb states that, *"If speaking is silver then listening is gold".* You can't go on the court thinking that you already know. It's when you think you already know you close yourself off from hearing and learning something new.

If you have a mentor or coach who's already 'Walk the Walk' then you should listen to them and learn. (I am really talking to myself here.) This part is tough if you think you already know it. Have you ever watched a movie the second time and see something you don't remember seeing the first time you saw the movie? It's like that! Always be open to listening, you will always learn something new. The Dalai Lama said it like this: *"When you talk, you are only repeating what you already know. But if you listen, you may learn something new."* Or as Jimi Hendrix said: *"Knowledge speaks, but wisdom listens."*

What's your next level?

Remember to play up, you can't be the brightest bulb in

your group and expect to grow and flourish. Surround yourself with people who know more than you. J. Paul Getty said: *"I'd rather have 1% of the effort of 100 men than 100% of my own effort."* I call this leverage! When I read this recently it took on a new meaning. I realize that if you want to build something you will eventually need a team. We first start off as a solopreneur, but if you really want to grow exponentially, then you will need a team to support you in the work you do.

Who can you learn from, so that you can play at the next level?

_____
_____
_____
_____
_____
_____
_____
_____
_____

Who do you need on your team?

_____
_____
_____
_____
_____
_____
_____
_____
_____
_____

Point 14
Own a Finish Strong Attitude

Set Up - a shot placing the ball in a great position for an aggressive offensive shot, often a kill shot.

> *There is no passion to be found playing small and settling for a life that is less than the one you are capable of living.*
> *Nelson Mandela*

Win or Lose, Finish Strong!

Win or lose you not only have to show up strong but finish strong! When you do this, you finish satisfied. You can't be disappointed if you gave it your all. Oftentimes we have a tendency of starting off strong but as the game continues, we get tired, we get bored, or we just may not have the stamina to finish what we've started. Most of the time this is when most people give up and throw in the towel.

My friend Monique told me about how her son would play football at the neighborhood park with his friends, however, when his team would be behind, he would take his football and leave the game! You can't just take your football and leave if the game does not go your way. You can never tell what the final outcome might yield. There have been many times when Serena Williams was behind in the game, however she continued to bring her 'A' game and, in most cases, she was victorious!

In the movie *'Night School'*, Kevin Hart played a character by the name of Teddy Walker who did not graduate from high school. He had to go back to earn his diploma to keep his job. He and his classmates decide to cheat on their exams. However, the teacher realized they cheated and had them all take the test over again. Everyone passed the test except Teddy. Although he kept taking the test again and again and again, each time he would fail. At the beginning he was upset and depressed about failing. However, his attitude around failing became more positive with each try. He had the AUDACITY NOT to give up. Teddy eventually passed the test and earned his diploma.

Imagine what could happen if you had the AUDACITY NOT to give up?

What might happen if you persist?

What might happen if you kept moving in that winning direction?

What could you accomplish?

My guess is that you will eventually succeed because you have the AUDACITY to not give up.

What does it look like to have the AUDACITY to not give up! It looks like you are persevering! Typically, people who give up easily assume that they can't win because of their circumstances, or a roadblock has them stuck. It's not that they can't achieve their goals. It may be that they may not have found their solution yet! They've got to keep on trying until they get the results they're seeking. It's an iterative process.

They've got to keep on moving forward. They may have to stop and reflect, maybe take a different approach, but **QUITTING IS NOT AN OPTION!** Like Nike said, "just **DO IT!**" Do it until the task is complete, and experience that game-winning hit. When they feel like quitting the most, that is when it is time to **TURN IT UP!**

DOn't Qu**IT**!

> "Age wrinkles the body but quitting wrinkles the soul."
> *Douglas MacArthur*

You Are Not the Only One Who is Tired.

Most likely your opponent is tired as well, but if you turn it up bringing new energy and momentum then you can win. You breathe life back into the game when your mind begins to believe that there is an opportunity to win.

Some of you may remember the fight between Muhammad Ali and George Foreman. This fight went down in the history books as the "Rumble in the Jungle". Both fighters were exhausted. Sweat poured from their bodies like faucets. By Round 7, it seemed as though they were going to go the distance. No one was quitting. But then came a turning point. Muhammad Ali began to use a technique never seen in boxing before. He began to do what is called the "Rope-a-dope". Ali protected his body and rested on the ropes as Foreman administered blow after blow to Ali's sweaty body. With each blow, Foreman's energy diminished, and out of nowhere Ali threw a right hook and the punch was felt around the world knocking George Foreman out. Ali took advantage of the situation and maintained the title of the heavyweight champion of the world! Ali used his will and maintained a finish strong attitude to win one of his most exhausting fights ever!

So, what does it look like to finish strong in your life? It looks like you putting in the time needed to succeed. Now I'm not saying that you have to put in an exorbitant number of hours all at one time, no you have to pace yourself! Schedule time for you to work on the things that are important. My dissertation advisor would always tell me to work on my paper for an hour or two and then take a half an hour break before getting back on track for the next 2 hours. I tried it and it actually worked! The thing is you have to be consistent! You can't start something and put it down for a couple of weeks and expect to jump back in with that same momentum. You have to keep the momentum by doing a little each day at a time. If you slip, get back in the game.

Finishing strong may look like you asking someone for support around something that is not your strength. This may allow you to focus on the things that are going to yield maximum profit.

- What steps do you need to take in order for you to finish strong?
- What help might you need in order for you to finish strong?
- How might you feel if you finished your goal strong?

The Real Secret

The secret to the lessons learned in this book is to believe in yourself! Believe that you are worthy!

> *"It does not matter how slowly you go as long as you don't stop."*
> Confucius

If you don't believe you're a winner or if you don't believe you will ever win then you are 100% RIGHT! I was inspired by the poem *'Pretty Ugly'* written by Abdullah Shoaib to write the poem below. Read the poem to yourself or out loud then answer the questions that follow.

I am NOT DESERVING
And you can't tell me
I am WORTHY

Because all I know is that
I LOSE at everything I try
And I'm not going to fool myself by saying
There is a WINNER in me
So best believe

I'll ALWAYS remind myself
That I'm NOT DESERVING
And nothing you can ever say will make me believe
I can WIN

Because no matter what you say
I am NOT WORTHY of abundance
And I am in no position to believe that
Abundance is my birthright

When I look in the mirror, I say to myself
Am I NOT DESERVING of my dreams?

- How might this person perceive themself?
- Where might they sit if they were to come into a room?
- What type of clothes might they wear?
- How would they stand or talk?
- In other words, how do they show up?

Now, I want you to read the poem again, but this time start from the bottom line and then read the previous line until you reach the top. Read it aloud so you can hear the words. Then answer the same question above.

The words in the poem did not change. You just reread it starting from the bottom to the top. In other words, it all depends on your perspective or shall we say, your position! It depends on where you stand as you read the poem! It all boils down to your point of view, your beliefs about who you are and who you be.

- Which position will you choose?
- Which position serves you the best?
- It's all up to you!
- Only you have the power to decide where you position yourself.

"Know that you are UNSTOPPABLE, you can do it, and you have what it takes. You need to believe in your strength, believe in your ability, and don't say no to you."
Serwa Kenyetta

Point 15

Win the Game

Then Create a New One
#PIVOT #CHANGE the Game

Bye - a guaranteed pass into the next round of a tournament, usually awarded to the top ranked players to allow them to bypass the first round without having to play a game.

Server – the player hitting the serve; the only player who can score.

If you create the game, then you create the rules.
And if you just, be you. There's no way you can lose.
India Arie

You are now the server at this point!

Know the Limitations, Parameters, and Norms, Then Create Your Own.

Sometimes the rules don't always apply, you may have to break the rules or change them. Stay with me here. If you are around Millennials, you know what I mean. They are in a different world with different philosophies, many of them are social and digital natives navigating technology, trading in the Forex market, texting, and painting their nails all at the same time! These young creators are leveraging their social media skills to become profitable entrepreneurs.

They don't play by our rules, just like we didn't play by our parents' rules. We lived in a different world than our parents. Our parents' world was during the time of factories and their philosophy was about staying on a job for thirty plus years and retire with a pension. They instilled in their children/us to do the same. That is, go to work for forty years, retire on 40% of our income, start taking out monies from our 401k's (that is going to be taxed) only to realize that we need another job because we can't maintain our current living status on that 40 percent!

Oprah talks about how her grandmother was grooming her to clean homes for rich white people. But something was pulling Oprah in a different direction. She knew deep down in her soul that she was not going to be cleaning homes. She trusted her intuition. Oprah decided to create her own rules, now look at her, she owns her own network!

Tell-A-Vision

You need to develop routines that serve you. Instead of watching tell-a-vision, you need to create-a-vision. Some of the things I do to help me create a vision is to write it out in words or draw ideas out as pictures in my vision journal. Every year I start a new journal to keep track of what I want to create and manifest for my future. Twice a year I hold a 'Design Your desired Destiny Playshop' to help others create a vision for the future.

Once you know what you want your future to look like, I highly recommend that you read books, take a course, be a part of a mastermind, hire a coach (I have three coaches now, a business coach, a writing coach, and my dissertation coach) or find a mentor that is already doing what you'd like to do (Also, NEVER hire a coach that does not have a coach for themself). Even Oprah has a coach.

Remember it's always key to do what you love so you can love what you do!
#PYGN

Your Thumbprint

There is no one in this world that has your exact thumbprint. During a Circle of Champions event, my mentor, Bob Yates would have someone come to the front of the room and write their name in cursive on the chart paper. Then he would ask another person to try to write that person's signature. No matter how many times the person tried, they could never repeat the person's signature. Bob wanted to prove that no one can do it quite the way you do it. That is, no one can do you better than you.

My friend Angie was making six-figures as the general manager of a major hotel establishment. She followed all the rules like a good girl. She went to school, got good grades, went to college, got a part time job while she was in college, and worked her way up from the kitchen all the way up the ladder to the general manager! Her mother was so proud of her, her family was proud of her, and her peers were all proud of her. Her life was good. Brain research shows that girls are more likely to follow the rules than boys.

Although Angie was successful, she was not happy at all. In fact, she was miserable! Every week during our coaching calls, she would complain about having to go to a job she hated. She was counting down the days before she would leave that job. Something was pulling her. So, when she quit her six-figure job to pursue her passion you can only imagine what her friends and family may have said. They probably said things like:

"Girl, you are crazy to quit your good job!"

"Have you lost your mind?"

"Who will pay your health benefits?"

"How will you pay your bills?"

"How are you going to pay your mortgage?"

"Why would you leave?"

"You will lose your hotel discounts!"

Ang broke the rules to the game played by her parents,

peers, and friends. Because Angie hired a coach and got direction, she was able to play her own game and create her own rules! She knew what she wanted, and her 9 to 5 was not giving her the satisfaction she craved. It wasn't good enough. Good is the enemy of GREAT. As a result of Angie following her intuition. She now has more time to spend with her husband and son and no longer has to manage her time, she created time freedom and is using her talents and gifts to serve the world.

Ang chose her future; she now helps people build their brand and she loves what she does. She is creating her life by design and not by default. Her road isn't easy by any means, but she is doing it! Mark Twain said, *"The two most important days in your life is the day you are born and the day you find out why."* Angie is finding out why she was born. She is no longer counting down the days before she can leave that job, she is now making her days count! She has created something to call her own, it has her fingerprints all on it, her unique signature. Angie would often say "being an entrepreneur is not for punks!"

Know the rules, play by the rules, and for those of you who prefer playing outside the boundaries, CHANGE THE GAME AND CREATE NEW RULES!

> *"Know the rules well, so you can break them effectively."*
> Dalai Lama

Work for You!

The shift from being an employee to becoming an entrepreneur may not be an easy feat for some. Some people are meant to be employees but for some of us, we are meant to be entrepreneurs. You can always spot them, they tend to start early babysitting, selling candy to their classmates, cutting the grass or shoveling the snow in the neighborhood. These natural entrepreneurs may have seen their parents or neighbors have a hustle whereas some entrepreneurs possess an innate unction to have their own. Some people learn they have entrepreneur skills later in life.

I started in elementary school cleaning houses like my mom. In high school I started selling Mary Kay. My architecture teacher, Mr. Kuo introduced me to Amway! I knew I wanted to be an entrepreneur. However, I was taught to go to school, get good grade so I can go to college and then get a "good government job".

Growing up, I don't remember seeing many entrepreneurs. Actually, let me take that back, I saw plenty of entrepreneurs in my neighborhood, unfortunately they engaged in non-legal activities.

When you are an entrepreneur, you have to work just as hard for your dream. We were trained from elementary school to go to a building from 9 to 3 and work. We were trained as children to turn in our work to our teachers, and as an adult, we are trained to turn in our work to our employers. And we do. We make sure we turn in our work on time. Meeting each deadline, sometimes working late at night. We have a schedule, and we stick to it because we want to keep our good jobs. However, sometimes when we work for ourselves, we neglect making a schedule to stay on track. We need to work just as hard if not harder for ourselves, our families, and our dreams. It requires discipline, do some long-range planning create a realistic schedule, and then stick to it! Remember what my friend Angie said "being an entrepreneur is not for punks".

Know Your 'Y'

Quick math lesson:

In math the 'Y' stands for your solution, your results. The 'Y' is the dependent variable.

Stay with me here. I know a lot of you may be thinking. I hate math or what does math have to do with this. Let me remind you, I am bringing all of myself to the table. Even the geeky math part! That makes me uniquely different from all the other coaches out there. Where was I? oh yes, dependent variables. For example: Your paycheck depends on the time you work.

If you are an entrepreneur, your income depends on your ability to enroll or persuade people to invest in your product or service.

Your health depends on what you eat or don't eat. Your mindset depends on your experience, who you surround yourself with, what you read and many other things. In other words, there are many variables that impact your mindset.

Therefore, your 'Y' is the outcome or output, it is the

results you get i.e., paycheck, health, and mindset. Your health powers you to monitor what you eat. You wanting to **'be fly until you die'** powers you to get up before the baby and get your workout on! Your mindset powers your ability to continue to grind, persevere, stay the course.

Your **'Y'** powers everything you do!

Last Question…

What is your 'Y' for Playing Your Game NOW?

The Hit List

1. Trust yourself!

2. Seize the moment!

3. Grant yourself permission!

4. Dawn your own mask, so you can help others.

5. Do what really makes you happy!

6. Embrace your uniqueness, be who you were made to be.

7. Measure yourself against you. Improve daily. One step at a time.

8. Hang out with people who value you and the gifts you bring.

9. Handle your business!

10. Spend time with positive people who match and give you energy!

11. Learn from your mistakes, they help you grow.

12. Take the time to enjoy and learn from the process, for it is the most valuable part of the journey.

13. Celebrate the success of others, your turn is next!

14. Your happiness lies within. It's within your power to choose how you want to feel.

15. Focus your energy on what you want.

This is your work, YOU have to

Live it!

Sleep it!

Breathe it!

Get engrossed in YOUR DREAMS

Made in the USA
Monee, IL
25 September 2021